Still
Hopeful

Still Hopeful

*LESSONS FROM
A LIFETIME
OF ACTIVISM*

Maude Barlow

Published by ECW Press
665 Gerrard Street East
Toronto, Ontario, Canada M4M 1Y2
416-694-3348 / info@ecwpress.com

Editor for the press: Susan Renouf
Copy editor: Jennifer Knoch
Cover design: Natalie Olsen

LIBRARY AND ARCHIVES CANADA CATALOGUING
IN PUBLICATION

Title: Still hopeful : lessons from a lifetime
of activism / Maude Barlow.

Names: Barlow, Maude, author.

Identifiers: Canadiana (print) 20210362634 |
Canadiana (ebook) 20210362642

ISBN 978-1-77041-632-1 (softcover)
ISBN 978-1-77305-934-1 (ePub)
ISBN 978-1-77305-935-8 (PDF)
ISBN 978-1-77305-936-5 (Kindle)

Subjects: LCSH: Barlow, Maude. | LCSH:
Social justice. | LCSH: Environmental
justice. | LCSH: Social reformers—
Canada—Biography.

Classification: LCC HM671 .B37 2022 | DDC
303.3/72—dc23

This book is funded in part by the Government of Canada. *Ce livre est financé en partie par le
gouvernement du Canada.* We acknowledge the support of the Canada Council for the Arts. *Nous
remercions le Conseil des arts du Canada de son soutien.* We acknowledge the support of the Ontario
Arts Council (OAC), an agency of the Government of Ontario, which last year funded 1,965 individual artists and 1,152 organizations in 197 communities across Ontario for a total of $51.9 million.
We also acknowledge the support of the Government of Ontario through Ontario Creates.

PRINTED AND BOUND IN CANADA

PRINTING: FRIESENS   5   4   3   2   1

To my grandchildren,
Madelaine, Eleanor, Angus and Max.

And to all the grandchildren of the world.

When you are tired, learn to rest, not to quit.

BANKSY

CONTENTS

INTRODUCTION

i thank You God for this most amazing
day: for the leaping greenly spirits of trees
and a blue true dream of sky; and for everything
which is natural which is infinite which is yes

E.E. CUMMINGS

I have been contemplating the notion of hope for a long time. I have been a social justice activist for over 40 years and have found hope to be a prerequisite for creating change and inspiring others. Hope has been built into the DNA of my life.

I come from a family dedicated to social justice. My father was a pioneer in the field of criminal justice and led the fight against capital and corporal punishment in Canada. I have an early memory of watching him debate Canada's official hangman on black-and-white TV. Canada's hangmen were always known as Mr. Ellis, and they wore a hood to disguise their features.

With our morning oatmeal, my two sisters and I were taught that we owed something for the privilege of living in a place of such opportunity. We were taught that hope is a moral imperative, and it has been my lifelong mantra.

Recently, however, it has been getting harder to remain hopeful against the relentless tide of negative information that threatens to drown us in a sea of despair. It is hard to pass a day that we don't read of more fires, hurricanes and drought, each year hotter than the one before; the mass melting of the planet's ice cover; the sixth great extinction; the devastation of insects, bees and birds; the destruction of rainforests and watersheds. We are entering a time of great economic uncertainty and devastating hardship for many millions of our fellow humans. Even before COVID exacted its terrible toll, the UN announced that three-quarters of the world's workers are in precarious jobs, without pensions, security or even a livable wage. Now, with whole industries collapsing and countries facing alarming drops in their GDPs, fear is setting in for those who face a compromised future.

In my social justice work, it is getting harder to stay positive in front of my colleagues, many of whom are such experts in the details of the crises we face that it is hard for them to offer hope themselves.

The idea for this book came to me on a lovely June evening in 2019 in a packed Ottawa church. I was on a panel about the Green New Deal with David Suzuki, Avi Lewis and a few others. Some spoke in language that I can only describe as apocalyptic, the message hammered home that there are only ten years left of a habitable planet. I noted that there were a lot of young people in the audience, including my 16-year-old granddaughter Eleanor.

In my presentation, I spoke of hope and about building movements and offered examples of winning campaigns.

This elicited some debate from the other panelists and a caution from Suzuki that we do not sugarcoat the facts. I have known, admired and worked with David for years and have watched him become increasingly and understandably frustrated with the glacial pace of change in the face of a worsening environmental crisis. Long a beacon of hope himself, he was angry this spring evening — as were we all — that the federal Liberal government had recently bought a pipeline and the NDP/Green coalition government of his home province of British Columbia was going ahead with the infamous Site C dam and an expanded fracking industry. Hope was in short supply in that Ottawa church.

After the event, a high school student came up to me in tears and thanked me for my hopeful words, saying she and her friends had sat devastated and paralyzed throughout the panel discussion until I spoke. What could they do in the face of such overwhelming evidence of ecological collapse, she asked. I had many ideas. On my walk home, the air fragrant with apple blossoms and lilac trees and the evening too lovely to feel anything but joy, I made a vow to help that young woman, and my grandkids, to find the path ahead.

How could I share what I have learned — including all the mistakes — in over 40 years of fighting for social and environmental justice? Do I and others of my generation have something to offer individuals and organizations working in equality, justice, democracy and environmental protection? Could we inspire young people to see that the life of an activist is a good life, one that gets you up in the morning thinking about more than yourself? Could we help arm them for the hard work and many disappointments ahead? Could we help them find the joy in the struggle to make a better world? Could we help them not to be overwhelmed with the enormity of the task ahead?

Standing under a newly leafed tree silvered by a new moon, I remembered the words of a PEI farmer friend who always said that when he is overwhelmed, he stops thinking of the enormity of the challenges he is facing and instead asks himself one simple question: What is the next appropriate step to take? Then he takes it.

Well, for me, the next appropriate step to take was to write this book. I offer it to you, with hope.

CHAPTER ONE

GIVE HOPE A CHANCE

Do not be daunted by
the enormity of the world's grief.
Do justly, now.
Love mercy, now.
Walk humbly, now.
You are not obligated to complete the work
But neither are you free to abandon it.

THE TALMUD

Coming out of a global pandemic and facing many crises, we need hope. Hope may not be for oneself, it may be for one's children, or one's children's children. This is the story of so many immigrants and refugees who suffer great hardships in search of a new life for their families. But hope can also be for other people's children and for the human family. Hope often defies logic and gives us the strength to continue when all the "facts" tell us things are hopeless. Hope helps us to put one foot in front of the other when despair would tell us not to move.

My fear is that the sense of hopelessness many people now feel makes them think that the situation itself is hopeless, leading to paralysis. In writing this book, I asked myself, What is hope? How has it sustained me through my life as an activist, and what lessons have I learned about the role of hope in my work? *Still Hopeful* is my best advice on how to keep hope alive, as Martin Luther King Jr. entreated us to do.

Distinguish between real and false hope

To start, I want to be clear that when I speak of hope, I am not talking about uninformed optimism — what Plato called "gullible" hope. The ancient Greeks warned of the danger of espousing hope based on insufficient knowledge that could lead to poor decisions in war and politics. This is not a call for cheerful optimism nor a denial of the urgent issues that we collectively face. Certainly I have done my share of disseminating the distressing facts and statistics on the climate crisis and in particular the threat to the world's water.

In his groundbreaking three-volume work, *The Principle of Hope*, published in the 1950s, the great German philosopher Ernst Bloch saw all of human history as the story of hope for a better future. Deeply marked by the two world wars and the class struggles and divisions within his own country, Bloch distinguished between what he called "fraudulent" or "false" hope and "genuine" hope, which, to be effective, needs to be stoked by "informed discontent." False hope, he warned, is often used by governments to tamp down dissent among the marginalized and can find us staring at a blank wall, blind to "the door that may be close."

American Zen Buddhist teacher Joan Halifax clarifies how she sees the difference between optimism and hope. Optimism, she says, can be dangerous as it doesn't require engagement. Things will be better on their own, says the optimist, and if they aren't, one can become a pessimist, taking refuge in the belief that there is nothing to be done. Optimists and pessimists actually have something in common, says Halifax — they are excused from engagement. She calls instead for "wise" hope, and wise hope most surely requires engagement.

Wise hope is born of radical uncertainty.

— JOAN HALIFAX

Joan Halifax has led an extraordinary life of service to what might be called "hopeless" situations, including ministering to the dying in hospices and men on death row. She is clear that hope is not the belief that everything will turn out well. After all, as she says, people die. Populations die out. Civilizations die. Stars die.

In a paper delivered at a 2019 conference in Australia, Halifax said that wise hope is born of radical uncertainty, rooted in the unknown and the unknowable. Wise hope requires that we open ourselves to what we do not know, what we cannot know, and to being perpetually surprised. Wise hope embraces the possibility of transformation and the understanding that what we do matters, even though how and when it will matter, who and what it may impact, are not things we can know beforehand.

Don't tie hope or success to a preordained outcome

Many times in this book, I am going to speak of the need to build movements, and the need for movements to have concrete goals and plans. Without a vision of what we want, it is hard to get others on board for the cause. Long-term goals are, in fact, essential to a purposeful movement and keep people from running in circles. But it is crucial not to judge the success of a campaign or struggle solely by an achievement within a hoped-for time frame. Successful campaigns can take a long time. As well, situations change, and we have to be able to adjust our expectations and refine the goals. Being too rigid will lead to disappointment and burnout. And it will kill hope.

Vandana Shiva, Indian scholar, environmental activist and food sovereignty expert, is very clear about how hope keeps her going and it isn't by "winning" everything she sets out to do. She has learned never to allow herself to become overwhelmed by hopelessness, no matter how tough the situation. She advises us to do our part without thinking of the scale of what we stand against; by tackling what we face, we enlarge our own capacities and create new potential. She has learned to detach herself from the results of what she does because those results are not in her hands.

"The context is not in your control, but your commitment is yours to make," she wrote me in an email. "And you can make the deepest commitment with total detachment about where it will take you. You want it to lead to a better world, and you shape your actions and take full responsibility for them. But then you have to have detachment. And that combination of deep passion and deep detachment allows me always to take on the next challenge because I don't tie myself up in knots."

Shiva mirrors the thinking of Mahatma Gandhi who said, "I am content with the doing of the task in front of me. I do not worry about the why and wherefore of things. Reason helps us to see that we should not dabble in things we cannot fathom."

Canadian philosopher and social theorist Brian Massumi says, in fact, the only way a concept like hope can be made useful is when it is not only connected to a desired success but is also rooted in the present. In an interview with Australian philosopher and writer Mary Zournazi for her 2003 book, *Hope: New Philosophies for Change*, he argues that uncertainty can be empowering once we realize that it gives us a margin of manoeuvrability and an opening through which to experiment. "The present's 'boundary condition,' to borrow a phrase from science, is never a closed door. It is an open threshold — a threshold of potential. You are only ever in the present in passing. You may not reach the end of the trail but at least there is a next step. The question of which next step to take is a lot less intimidating than how to reach a far-off goal in a distant future where all our problems will finally be solved," he writes.

Ernst Bloch admitted that even a well-founded hope can be disappointed, otherwise it would not be hope. In a 1961 public lecture at the University of Tübingen, Germany, he said, "In fact, hope never guarantees anything. It is characteristically daring and points openly to possibilities that in part depend on chance for their fulfilment." Hope can learn and become smarter through roadblocks, but true hope can never be driven off course.

Because we do not live in the world we aspire to, we do not have the experience to formulate that world completely. "Still," Bloch said, "it is possible to determine the direction toward real humanism, a direction that is invariable and unconditional; it is indicated precisely in the oldest conscious dream of humankind — in the overthrow of all conditions in which the human individual is a humiliated, enslaved, forsaken, despised creature."

In fact, hope never guarantees anything. It is characteristically daring and points openly to possibilities that in part depend on chance for their fulfilment.

— ERNST BLOCH

I have learned from my own work and through watching other activists that in thinking you can control the outcome of a campaign or action, you are probably giving yourself too much credit. You will also be setting yourself up for burnout. It is absolutely essential to trust that others are doing their part and, in ways you cannot know, are inspiring change.

Vi Morgan was a writer, storyteller and activist living and fighting for justice in Guelph, Ontario. Along with her husband, retired pioneer educator Griff Morgan, she ran the local chapter of the Council of Canadians and led the campaign to keep Walmart out of her city. They succeeded for over a decade. At an anti-Walmart public forum in 2004, Griff Morgan gave an impassioned speech to great applause about the importance of preserving the downtown core and protecting local business. Then, right there, speech finished, in front of young and old, he dropped dead. The next day, the *Guelph Mercury* had a front-page photo of Vi and Griff and me with a quip from the mayor, saying, "Now heaven is safe from Walmart."

The last time I visited Vi was in May 2015, just weeks before she died at the age of 100. Her brain still sharp, she asked me if I had a "quiet mind." What a canny and observant question! If I struggle with anything, it is letting go. I want always to heed my own advice to detach from the outcome, but it is hard for me. I hate losing and get frustrated with the slow pace of change. Why aren't others upset at this? What can I do to make them care? What will it take to make change? Vi took my hands in both of hers and told me that I would find my quiet mind when I truly understand that others are, in fact, doing important things I cannot know about and when I learn to trust a greater force present in humanity.

American scholar and professor John Paul Lederach is known the world over for his work on peacekeeping and mediation. He has travelled into many of the worst conflict zones to broker peace agreements, sometimes putting his own life in peril. In a 2014 interview for *Sojourners Magazine*, he spoke of his Mennonite faith and how it has guided him when peace missions have failed. He said that he chooses to live according to a vision of relationships, community and creation as if they were possible even when all the signs around him suggest they are not. "Hope is love lived," he said. "Even in deep disappointment, you don't stop the heartbeat of love.

Love requires patience and humility, reaching out, noticing the small gifts and the presence of life around you . . . When disappointment hits, remember you are a child of God, loved and nurtured. Just think of the breath of air you are taking right now, it is a gift. Remember the world does not rotate around you or depend on whether you were successful. Don't serious yourself to death. Be kind to yourself. Find a park, find some children and remember how to play. Smile. Take a walk in the woods. Watch a flower in the sun for half an hour and think about unrequited beauty."

In American activist and public intellectual Rebecca Solnit's 2004 book, *Hope in the Dark*, she echoes this notion that we cannot know what will make a difference. Yes, she posits, the future is dark, but it is inscrutable, not necessarily terrible. Many transform this unknowability into something certain and awful, the "fulfillment of their dread." She gently reminds us, "Far stranger things happen than the end of the world."

She writes, "That is because we do not see the myriad of changes happening in the area of human rights and justice, for example, that would have been thought impossible only decades ago. The world is wilder than our imaginations. Causes and effects assume history marches forward, but history is not an army. It is a crab scuttling sideways, a drip of soft water wearing away stone, an earthquake breaking centuries of tension. Sometimes one person inspires a movement, or her words do decades later; sometimes a few passionate people change the world; sometimes they start a mass movement and millions do; sometimes those millions are stirred by the same outrage or the same ideal and change comes upon us like a change of weather."

Face the reality of our situation

Greta Thunberg says that, upon learning about the climate crisis at age 11, she fell into a deep depression and stopped talking and even eating, losing 22 pounds in two months. She didn't start to emerge from her depression until, at age 15, she decided to act by sitting in front of the Swedish Parliament every day rather than going to school. As we know, she went on to inspire a global youth climate revolution. Action was her cure. "When we start to act, hope is everywhere. So, instead of looking for hope — look for action. Then the hope will come," she argues.

. . . but history is not an army. It is a crab scuttling sideways . . .
— REBECCA SOLNIT

But not all young people have been able to find an outlet for their fears as they learn about the multiple environmental crises in their classrooms and from the media. Many educators and psychologists working with young people are reporting a dramatic increase in pessimism and fear in their charges. A September 2020 *Washington Post*–Kaiser Family Foundation poll of American teenagers found that almost 60% said that climate change made them feel scared and over half said it made them feel angry. The American Academy of Pediatrics issued a policy statement in 2015 warning that the climate crisis poses a threat to children's mental and physical health and that failure to take prompt substantive action would be an "act of injustice to all children."

In expert testimony for a 2018 lawsuit filed by a group of young people seeking to force the US government to adopt policies to fight the climate crisis, Washington-based psychiatrist Lise Van Susteren wrote that children will be at the centre of the storm as climate change worsens. "Day in and day out worrying about the unprecedented scale of the risk posed by climate change takes a heavy toll on an individual's well-being, wearing them down, sending some to the 'breaking point.' Children are especially vulnerable." She told the *Washington Post* that interviewing children about their fears for nature and their future families left her with a "sense of shame."

In his 2020 book, *Commanding Hope: The Power We Have to Renew a World in Peril*, University of Waterloo professor Thomas Homer-Dixon cites studies showing that pessimism about the economic future of young people is "widespread" in most countries, although the shift in attitude since the beginning of the millennium has been particularly stark in Western countries. Homer-Dixon says that it is imperative that we name and face the four "enormous social earthquakes" our societies are facing in the coming decades as these "hard-to-see, slow-moving and diffuse tectonic stresses steadily build in force, cross social boundaries and scales, and combine to multiply their effects."

The first is rising economic inequality and economic insecurity and a fear that one's basic economic well-being

Wenonah Hauter

Wenonah Hauter is an environmental organizer and author. She is founder and executive director of Food & Water Watch, a grassroots movement of over one million Americans working for food, water and energy rights.

Where do you find hope?

"Recent times have been difficult as people have been ravaged by the COVID-19 pandemic, a brutal economy and climate change–supercharged fires, hurricanes and floods. In the United States, underlying these disasters is a fractured democracy and a highly polarized and divided country. In this context, it is easy to feel dejected and hopeless. Still, I remain remarkably hopeful for the future.

"I'm hopeful because of how I see people responding. I draw hope from an inspired and bold movement of young people who are expecting more from their leaders. I draw hope from the growing climate justice movement. I draw hope from the growing number of people who recognize and are fighting for the right to water. I am hopeful because we are making progress in our fight to create a fair and healthy food system. And I draw hope from the rising movement for racial, social, economic and environmental justice that is powering all these changes.

"People often quote Martin Luther King's speech where he said 'the arc of the moral universe is long, but it bends towards justice.' But progressive change is not inevitable: we are the ones who bend the arc — ordinary people standing up, organizing and demanding a world that embraces justice. I'm hopeful because I see a new boldness and audacity in the demands by a wider segment of our country. And I'm hopeful because I see the real progress this work is bringing about. Racial, social, economic and environmental justice are urgent and pressing. We must continue to work for the world we want and deserve."

could abruptly change for the worse. The second is the growing movement of people, chiefly economic migrants and refugees, from areas of the world where life is terribly hard and dangerous to areas where it could be better. They may be fleeing terrorism or state-sponsored violence or declining access to food, water and soil. The third, of course, is the climate crisis, what Homer-Dixon calls a "stealth threat" to people's feelings of security, possibility and hope.

The fourth social earthquake is called "normative threat" and arises when people see change — in their income, status or social or cultural norms — as a threat to their way of life. International polls show many people worry that the familiar touchstones of their lives and the essential fabric of their culture, moral values and shared beliefs are being torn apart rapidly. One can dismiss the last factor as the work of small-minded or right-wing people who don't want to share power, but it is important in understanding the susceptibility to conspiracy theories and disinformation in otherwise seemingly rational people. Something is threatening their way of life and they are vulnerable to those who say the changes may not be benign.

These "earthquakes" have led to a shift in the social mood of people, says Homer-Dixon, and a loss in confidence of a positive future. An astonishing 82% of people surveyed worldwide by Ipsos think we live in an increasingly dangerous world. *New York Times* conservative columnist and cultural commentator David Brooks writes that this shift in mood is from one of an "abundance mindset," where there is enough for all, to one of a "scarcity mindset," where resources are limited, the world is dangerous and group conflict is inevitable. "It's us versus them. If they win, we're ruined, therefore let's stick with our tribe." This way lies division and conflict.

Accept the need to grieve

Holding on to hope in the face of these "social earthquakes" requires that we face them squarely. This does not mean that we need to think about them all the time or drown ourselves in one terrible report of human suffering or environmental disaster after another. But accepting the reality of our situation is crucial, as is listening to the words of scientists and experts so that we do not take the wrong path. We must start from a place of knowledge and open our hearts and minds to the issues we face and the suffering of others.

Jamie Kneen is the executive director of MiningWatch Canada. He deals almost daily with atrocities committed by mining companies or their thugs in the Global South. He says that in answer to the question "How do you keep going?" he usually talks about the courage of the activists on the ground in those countries. But in an email to me he added, "I also think handling grief is important, for however positive and exciting new developments may be, or how resilient Nature really is, the losses are so massive, whether at a personal level or all the way to the biodiversity level, as to overwhelm."

In her 1986 book, *Selected Poems II*, Margaret Atwood wrote, "The facts of this world, seen clearly / are seen through tears; why tell me then / there is something wrong with my eyes?" Or as climate activists say, "If you're not worried, you're not paying attention."

David Suzuki argues that the tragedy we are witnessing in so many places around the world is heartbreaking and requires us to ask what we should do with our suffering. In a December 2015 commentary for the *Georgia Straight*, he writes that the way we deal with our pain has critical implications and warns that violence is what we get when we don't know what else to do. It can be projected outward in hate or discrimination, violence and even war, or absorbed inward in despair and self-destruction.

Suzuki should know about overcoming hate. When he was six years old, his family was stripped of their possessions and sent to an internment camp for people of Japanese heritage. It was the height of the Second World War and at least 21,000 Japanese Canadians were forcibly removed from their homes without any charge or due process and exiled to remote areas of British Columbia. Many were deported. Suzuki's family of five was relocated from Vancouver to the Slocan Valley, where they lived in one room in a dirty, rundown hotel and where their fourth baby was born. After the war, the family was forced to leave their beloved British Columbia and move to a small town in Ontario, where they were the only visible-minority family.

Suzuki says he learned three important lessons from this experience. The first is that it is easy to live up to ideals, such as everyone having equal rights in a democracy when times are easy. But it is when times are tough that these ideals are truly put to the test. The second is that he learned to hate bigotry in all its forms and sees the struggles for equality and justice of others as his own. The third is that sharing and speaking openly about the pain he experienced and the lessons he learned from this time has helped him heal and given him hope that it can do the same for others.

"Instead of knee-jerk reactions that so often accompany fear and emotional pain," writes Suzuki, "what if we summoned the courage to experience our sadness, disorientation, and grief in all its fullness? More importantly, what if we did this together? The feelings surrounding change and loss highlight our shared vulnerability and expose our connections to one another. We can consciously foster a heightened sense of human and ecological fellowship." Don't rush past feelings, Suzuki cautions. Take time to share and understand them and then use them to come together in the best humanity has to offer.

Kate Marvel would agree. She is a respected climate scientist with the NASA Goddard Institute for Space Studies at Columbia University. Referring to what has already been wrought by the climate crisis, she wrote in a March 2018 post for *On Being*, "I have no hope that these changes can be reversed. We are inevitably sending our children to live on an unfamiliar planet. But the opposite of hope is not despair. It is grief. Even while resolving to limit the damage, we can mourn. And here, the sheer *Grief is not* scale of the problem provides a perverse com- *despair.* fort: we are in this together. The swiftness of the change, its scale and inevitability, binds us into one, broken hearts trapped together under a warming atmosphere . . . Grief after all is the cost of being alive."

Overcome despair and face fear

Grief is not despair. Grief can lead to understanding, acceptance and engagement. Despair leads to a dead end.

Clarissa Pinkola Estés is an American poet, post-trauma specialist, Jungian psychoanalyst and the author of many books, including the bestselling *Women Who Run with the Wolves*. She urges us not to "spend your spirit dry by bewailing these difficult times," no matter how righteous our rage. In a spring 2020 public message called "Letter to a Young Activist During Troubled Times," Estés asks us to embrace these difficult times exactly because we were made for them. "For years," she says, "we have been learning, practicing, been in training for and just waiting to meet on this exact plain of engagement.

"In any dark time, there is a tendency to veer toward fainting over how much is wrong or unmended in the world. Do not focus on that. There is a tendency too to fall into being weakened by perserverating on what is outside your reach, by what cannot yet be. Do not focus there. That is spending the wind without raising the sails." Estés admits that she has felt despair many times in her life, "but I do not keep a chair for it; I will not entertain it. It is not allowed to eat from my plate."

Despair can be countered by action, however small. "We are needed, that is all we can know . . . Ours is not the task of fixing the entire world all at once, but of stretching out to mend the part of the world that is within our reach. Any small, calm thing that one soul can do to help another soul, to assist some portion of this poor suffering world, will help immensely. It is not given to us to know which acts or by whom, will cause the critical mass to tip toward an enduring good."

For many people, the knowledge that real hope demands action creates fear. What can I do? What if I am not a leader? What if I speak up and say something stupid? What if I advise the wrong thing? What do I have to add? Who will listen to me? Will I be in harm's way? Am I brave enough?

Elin Kelsey is a Canadian environmental scholar, educator and public speaker. In her 2020 book, *Hope Matters: Why Changing the Way We Think Is Critical to Solving the Environmental Crisis*, she says that the culture of fear that has grown up around the climate crisis is paralyzing for many, especially the young. Badgering someone you love will not change them, she writes, and bombarding kids with messages of gloom and telling them it is up to them to save the world with little support for how those messages make them feel is a recipe for paralysis. She reports that the messaging — from mainstream media and from academics and environmental groups — is largely centred on the crisis and not the solutions. By focusing on what is broken, messages about climate change make people feel that nothing has been done and that all the hard work lies ahead.

Kelsey strongly disagrees with that framing. When fear becomes the frame and the mindset, it is demotivating and can lead to compassion fatigue. "When we are afraid, we become less creative, less collaborative and less capable of perseverance. And that's where the paradox comes in. As a global community, with climate concern at a record high, we are better positioned than ever before to take urgently needed action, yet the collateral damage on individual people of being constantly bombarded with environmental catastrophe is inhibiting our capacity to tackle the climate crisis," she writes. Conversely, there is an essential connection between hope and agency. Kelsey points to studies that show hopeful people have the ability to find many routes to a goal, a skill that can be taught. "In other words, we could shape our hopeful future and we could be taught how to do so."

In her 2010 poem "Five Fears to Fear, and Then, No More," Estés writes, "going over and over one's fears / is empty / and emptying." Most fear, she writes, is not of failure of living fully. She advises choosing your petty fears carefully for they can grow big teeth. "Fear these: Fear not loving / while you have the chance. / Fear becoming bitter. / Fear cynicism. / Fear turning to stone. / Fear living underwhelmed by everything."

Rebecca Solnit believes that fear can be conquered by risk. "To hope is to gamble," she writes in *Hope in the Dark*. "It's to bet on the future, on your desires, on the possibility that an open heart and uncertainly is better than gloom and safety. To hope is dangerous, and yet it is the opposite of fear, for to live is to risk. . . . Hope should shove you out the door! . . . To hope is to give yourself to the future, and that commitment to the future makes the present inhabitable."

Even in the face of very stark evidence of environmental destruction, there are powerful voices calling for hope. The stunning summer 2021 report from the UN's

Intergovernmental Panel on Climate Change made apocalyptic headlines around the world and left many activists filled with despair. But one of the lead scientists on the project called on us all to use the shocking information in the report to turn the situation around. In an August 2021 editorial in *The Guardian*, Australian climate scientist Joëlle Gergis shared how hard she and 233 other volunteer scientists from 66 countries worked thousands of hours to produce the most comprehensive report on the climate crisis to date. Why did they do this? Because, Gergis said, they care.

To hope is to give yourself to the future, and that commitment to the future makes the present inhabitable.

— REBECCA SOLNIT

"Many of us realise that we are the generation that is likely to witness the destabilisation of the Earth's climate; that the people alive today will determine the fate of humanity. Being part of a group of scientists from every corner of the world working together to try to avert disaster at this critical moment in human history, changed my life. It taught me that when we align behind a collective vision guided by strong leadership — no matter how insurmountable the challenges feel — anything is possible.

"Ultimately, we only really have one choice to make — to stay connected with people that restore our faith in the goodness of humanity, or fall into an abyss of cynicism and despair. It really is a simple as that. You can choose to be a person that restores someone else's faith in humanity, and do what you can where you can, even when all feels lost.

"Because once the despair has passed, we need to remember that there is still so much worth saving."

Stand in solidarity with those in danger around the world

I have dealt with fear more than despair, as I am by nature hopeful and look to the positive. But fear is an ever-present companion for activists. I cannot claim to understand the courage it takes for many of my friends and allies around the world to deal with the kind of opposition they face.

I have been tear-gassed. I was chased by police with batons in Hong Kong. I have been in the midst of a stun gun attack by police in Johannesburg. I was hosed with water cannons and body-slammed by a Turkish security guard in Istanbul. I have been arrested in my own country, on Parliament Hill in Ottawa. These experiences have given me a taste — just for a few hours — of what it is like to have your freedom removed. But I seldom have had to face the kind of visceral threat that so many encounter on a regular basis.

Cerro de San Pedro is a small village 10 kilometres from San Luis Potosí City, a Mexican state capital. It was founded 400 years ago as a mining town in north-central Mexico and its surroundings are pockmarked with abandoned mining sites from centuries of extraction. Opposition to a proposed reopening of an old mine site held up exploration for a decade, but by 2008, the Vancouver-based company New Gold was in full production of an open pit silver and gold mine so vast the area's only aquifer was at risk, its river polluted with mining tailings and most of its villagers relocated. The extraction process ran 24 hours a day, with tons of explosives detonated every day until the famous mountain for which the town was named was completely razed and the mine closed in 2016.

In 2013, I visited Cerro de San Pedro with Mexican human rights activist Claudia Campero, as part of a human rights tour of the area. I was stunned to see this haunting old colonial settlement with its two heritage churches dwarfed by the massive mine encroaching right up to the town square. Local activists told us of years of threats and intimidation, including beatings, by thugs reportedly paid by the company. As we walked through town, I felt that we were being followed, and our guides confirmed there were state security forces watching our every move. They had closed the mine with its light and noise pollution for our visit to make us believe they closed the mine every night.

When we got into our cars to leave, dusk had fallen and we had to take a country road to get to the main highway where there would be the relative safety of traffic. All the way along the darkened country road, we were followed by several black cars, and all I could think of was that we were going to be pulled over and hurt or "disappeared," as has happened to so many who defy injustice and brutality. That night, on that drive, I understood the fear that activists in so many parts of the world must live with.

Alex Neve served as secretary general of Amnesty International Canada for over 20 years. In his retirement message, he wrote that the world has, perhaps, never been so divided about respecting and upholding human rights, and the need to fight for human rights has never been more urgent. He spoke of his first Amnesty meeting at his university 35 years before, and how he was energized by its "be the change" message and its call to action. "Yes, it is a world full of deeply entrenched cruelty and injustice, which can easily seem insurmountable. But here is one step to take, one letter to write — right now — to begin to make a difference."

Neve shared his gratitude for the courage and conviction of those putting their lives on the line for justice and how they have inspired him to keep going. "There has been no greater gift over these two decades than to find common cause with and be led by incredible human rights defenders, survivors and families at the frontlines of repression and struggle around the world . . . For anyone who doubts that change is possible, for anyone who feels deflated by apathy or defeated by the powerful interests blocking progress, that is where hope, fueled by necessity, outrage and determination, has its home. More than anything else, it is their voices — often reassuring, sometimes enraged, frequently challenging, always clarion — that will stay with me."

If ever there was a strong case for hope, it is found in the fight for justice for those in danger around the world. Nothing makes me angrier than hearing people say from the relative safety and security of their home communities that they have "given up" because there is "no point." Hope is a moral imperative for those of us who have had the luck of living in places that are relatively safe or who are born into privilege by the colour of our skin or the financial situation of our families. I get upset hearing young scholars on elite campuses, their futures stretched out before them on a silver platter, bemoan the futility of trying to change things. Giving up hope for change is to condemn so many others to misery.

Untold millions are leaving their countries of birth due to hunger, terrorism or state violence. Millions live in countries ruled by bully-boy dictators who use torture and imprisonment to control their people. Many rot in prisons for their political views and many others work in sweatshops under horrible conditions. Indigenous people everywhere are in retreat, their sacred lands taken over by corporations searching for minerals, oil, biodiverse plants and the biggest trees. There is no more compelling reason for hope than the need for those of us who can make a difference to step forward and stand in solidarity with those suffering from or fighting these injustices. Our very humanity calls us to act.

Hope is a moral imperative for those of us who have had the luck of living in places that are relatively safe or who are born into privilege by the colour of our skin or the financial situation of our families.

Find hope in the power of the collective

In engaging, you will find a world of activists, people who get up in the morning thinking about something other than making a living or just looking after themselves. Many a time, I have stepped off a plane in a faraway place to be greeted by people I have never met but with whom I strike up an immediate bond because of our shared analysis of the issue we are working on and our activism. In this fellowship lies great joy.

Rudolf Amenga-Etego

Rudolf Amenga-Etego is a public interest lawyer, activist and former Ghanaian MP known for his successful fight against major water privatization in his country. He founded a pan-African movement against water privatization and currently serves as executive director of the Foundation for Grassroots Initiatives in Africa. For his courageous advocacy, he has been tortured, imprisoned and shot at.

Where do you find hope?

"The fight for water justice in my country was one of life and death as our people are poor and cannot afford private water. The most noble cause of our generation is to fight for public water, a clean environment and secure land. The successful struggle against the World Bank gave new impetus to our people to face other issues and threats. Accessible public water frees women and girl children to participate in their communities. What is more democratic than people taking control of their own lives by taking back water from private control?

"Now we face a new threat. Land grabbers have emerged and turned what has been common property accessible to all families into a tradable commodity priced beyond the pockets of the people. But we will take the lesson we learned from the water fight to protect the land. I grew up tilling the land. I understand the land. I know what hurts the land and what nourishes it. When the land is happy, I feel it. The fragile soil of my country fed my people for generations and I came to understand that it is an interdependent relationship. We take care of the soil and it takes care of us. We are in a struggle for the survival of our planet. Global solidarity is the solution. We can never accept a philosophy that puts profits before people."

Let me share with you what I have learned from 40 years of activism fuelled by hope — personal and collective. It is not about winning a particular cause or even a campaign. It is about building a movement that is sustainable. It is about democracy. It is about supporting one another through hard times. It is about laughter and good food together. It is about long hours driving to long meetings. It is about trust and friendship. It is about protecting all that is good for future generations and the planet. It is about commitment to a dream that is larger than any one of its parts.

We have to learn to see victory in small things: a new friend, an emerging network, information we didn't have before. And we have to recognize that sometimes our victories may come as subtle, complex, slow changes instead of the big wins we would like — and count them anyway.

I have learned it is always too soon to give up and also always too soon to go home.

Alex Neve says that whenever his spirits flagged, he sensed energy from colleagues down the hall, out on the street or halfway around the world. Whenever a friend has lost hope, others have come to the fore. He writes that he is forever awed by the power of people coming together, close to home and across the globe, and the unstoppable force for change that solidarity unleashes.

It is not about winning a particular cause or even a campaign. It is about building a movement that is sustainable.

"What is particularly rich," he writes in his retirement post, "is that everyone brings their own skills, perspective, and experience to the human rights struggle. Fastidious researchers, dynamic mobilizers, quiet workhorses, incredible pro bono lawyers, imaginative campaigners, eloquent communicators, loyal letter-writers, generous donors, and so much more. What you bring and who we are together, I will never leave behind."

When on May 1, 2016, a raging wildfire destroyed much of Fort McMurray in northern Alberta and forced the panicked evacuation of 88,000 people, Canadians raised over $60 million in donations in a week that were then matched by the federal government. Children across the country set up lemonade stands, and musicians held charity concerts. Families in Edmonton, Red Deer and Lethbridge opened their homes to the now homeless of Fort McMurray and hundreds of volunteers brought food, flowers and cheer to the Red Cross shelter in Edmonton. *Maclean's* said that the fire and its aftermath bound this "vast country" more tightly together. Similarly, during the worst of the summer/fall 2020 fires in California, thousands of volunteers provided food and shelter and distributed relief items for the more than 100,000 displaced people.

Perhaps one of the most moving stories of a collective response to an unexpected crisis took place in the little town of Gander, Newfoundland (population 10,000) on September 11, 2001, when 38 planes carrying nearly 7,000 passengers from 100 countries were forced to land there after the US closed its air space in the wake of the terrorist attack on the Twin Towers.

While the planes sat for many hours on the tarmac and then many more hours passed as passengers had to go through rigorous security clearance, the townspeople readied makeshift shelters in schools, gyms, community centres, churches and camps, and prepared food for their hungry, frightened and anxious guests. They took the passengers, many of whom had never heard of Newfoundland, far less Gander, sightseeing, moose hunting, berry picking and barbecuing. They brought them into their homes for showers and held nightly concerts of local music.

Out of this experience came lifelong friendships and a stunning musical called *Come from Away*. A September 11, 2017, story on this event in *USA Today* quoted American passenger Robert Steuber, stranded with his wife and elderly father-in-law, saying he was absolutely floored by the hospitality they received. "The whole community is the poster child for how hospitality and just a sheer act of humanity should be because they had such a high level of open arms, and 'come in and welcome and here's my house.'"

What is important to note in these examples and so many more is that no one stopped to ask if it was worth taking action. People didn't ask whether it was futile to act because there are bound to be more fires and more disasters. They didn't despair about the enormity of the crisis; they acted in the present. They responded to an immediate need with good cheer and, in doing so, created hope for themselves and those they helped.

The power of the collective is even greater in times of widespread crises, such as the climate crisis, species extinction, water shortages and forest depletion. Coming together to address these challenges is what Homer-Dixon calls a "tipping phenomenon." He says the COVID-19 pandemic that hit the world in early 2020 is a vivid example of how we can flip from one state to another extraordinarily quickly when needed.

He told the *Calgary Herald* in a September 2020 interview, "I think, conventionally, most of us see an incrementalist progression of changes in our lives. Tomorrow will be basically the same as yesterday, with maybe some slight shifting at the edges. But those of us that study complex systems know that all complex systems — whether they are ecological systems, global climate, financial systems, people's world views — have the capacity under certain circumstances to jump from one equilibrium to another, to flip really quickly. We did that, essentially globally, within a matter of a few weeks in March. . . . By early April, almost half the world's population — I've seen some estimates of four billion people — were essentially locked down. We have never seen something like that in the history of the human species." He says the pandemic has shown us that we have a shared fate, good or bad. He adds that this is the message for battling climate chaos and the other huge environmental threats of our time.

Rebecca Solnit agrees. In a March 2020 interview with Boston National Public Radio, she says that in disasters she has studied, she has been taken by the extraordinary "upwelling of ordinary people" reaching out to do what is needed to take care of each other. In doing so, they found a sense of joy and power and connection that had often been missing in their everyday lives. This can open doors to radical change. Many countries, including self-described democracies, deemphasize the power of ordinary people.

Oscar Olivera

*Oscar Olivera was a factory workers'
union leader in Cochabamba,
Bolivia, when in 1999 his government
and the World Bank came to a deal
to privatize the water system. He
helped launch a grassroots network
of opposition and spearheaded
a fierce and successful revolution
against the project.*

NOAH FRIEDSKY D.R., 2004

Where do you find hope?

"When the World Bank told our government to privatize our
water, we, the common people, created meeting spaces for neighbours, peasants, young people, workers, unemployed and others
to come together. There, we recognized values we had forgotten:
solidarity, respect, reciprocity, fraternity. We achieved an amazing
level of social equality as there was no recognition of leaders or
bosses. We created a space with which everyone could identify.

"During the hardest part of the struggle, I saw the people in
the streets standing up to the army, and it was their decision, their
strength and their rage that gave me the courage to keep going.
People firmly believed we were going to win and that was all I
needed to feel we should move forward, as our cause was just. One
day an elderly Indigenous woman came up to me at the barricades
and gave me a stick and told me that with this stick, I would lead
and we would win.

"From that water war, we not only recovered water for all,
we created new forms of social coexistence and human bonding.
We recovered trust in one another and that caused us to lose our
fear. When one loses fear, there is no force capable of stopping our
quest for justice."

But when a disaster like COVID-19 happens, the gaps in care are made evident and the chance for radical social transformation opens up. Social programs long thought to be impossible may come to pass. Financial desperation, homelessness and inequality can suddenly be addressed. But it is a contest, she warns, as the opportunities for a more egalitarian or a more authoritarian society burst out of the gate like racehorses.

"Every disaster shakes loose the old order," says Solnit. "The sudden catastrophe changes the rules and demands new and different responses, but what those will be are the subject of a battle. These disruptions shift people's sense of who they and their society are, what matters and what's possible, and lead, often, to deeper and more lasting change, sometimes to regime change. Many disasters unfold like revolutions; the past gives us many examples of calamities that led to lasting national change."

Remember the achievements that have come from past crises

We can't help but see things through the eyes of our own generation and to think that the threats we face are unique. But there are whole generations before us that have faced war, famine, enslavement, poverty and hunger — and emerged stronger.

The Second World War is an example of a disaster that shook loose the old order. The deadliest military conflict in history, during which humans visited upon one another unimaginable horrors, killed as many as 85 million people. Vowing "never again," 50 nations gathered in San Francisco in April 1945 to launch the United Nations, whose charter, ratified months later, set out the goals of maintaining international peace and security, developing friendly relations among nations and achieving international cooperation to solve international problems.

Now with 193 members, the mandate of the UN has expanded to deal with issues related to health care, the environment, criminal justice, refugees and migration and human rights. While it indisputably failed in some crucial conflicts over the years, the United Nations nevertheless has catalogued remarkable successes. It has provided food to 90 million people in over 75 countries and assisted more than 34 million refugees. It has authorized 71 international peacekeeping missions and worked with 140 nations in an effort to address the climate crisis. The UN assists about 50 countries every year with elections. It has led the international fight against HIV/AIDS and provided vaccinations for 58% of the world's children.

One of its greatest achievements was the ratification of the 1948 Universal Declaration of Human Rights, marking a watershed in the long international quest to assert the supremacy of human and citizen rights over political or economic tyranny of any kind. The declaration grants the fundamental human rights of freedom, equality, life, liberty and security to every person regardless of race, colour, religion, sex, language, political opinion, national or social origin, birth or other status. It bans slavery, torture, arbitrary arrest, detention and exile among many other far-reaching goals. Together with the International Covenant on Economic, Social and Cultural Rights and the International Covenant on Civil and Political Rights, the declaration stands as a modern-day Magna Carta.

Over time, other human rights resolutions and covenants would be adopted by the nations of the world. Protections for the rights of children (1959), women (1967) and refugees and migrants (2016) would be enshrined. In 2005, the UN Responsibility to Protect resolution required states to act against genocide, war crimes, ethnic cleansing and crimes against humanity.

The UN covenants bound state signatories to accept a moral and legal obligation to protect and promote the human and social rights granted to the peoples of the world by the Declaration of Human Rights. This was revolutionary thinking and came to represent the foundation stones of modern democracy.

Nothing has ever been achieved by the person who says, "It can't be done."
— ELEANOR ROOSEVELT

Eleanor Roosevelt, wife of wartime president Franklin D. Roosevelt, was an early delegate to the United Nations General Assembly and one of the chief architects of the Declaration of Human Rights. She used to say that hope is the most neglected word in language. "Surely, in the light of history, it is more intelligent to hope rather than to fear, to try rather than not to try. For one thing we all know beyond doubt: Nothing has ever been achieved by the person who says, 'It can't be done.'"

She also insisted that universal human rights begin in small places, close to home — "so close and so small that they cannot be seen on any maps of the world." The neighbourhoods where people live, the schools they attend, the factories or farms where they work, this is where the fight for equality and justice begins. "Unless these rights have meaning here, they have little meaning anywhere. Without concerned citizen action to uphold them close to home, we shall look in vain for progress in the larger world."

Of course, abuses did not stop with the declaration. Torture still exists. Refugees live in horrific conditions and racism and violence are still with us. Nevertheless, humanity took an evolutionary step forward with the adoption of the Universal Declaration of Human Rights and set the foundation for the intense struggles for racial and social justice to come.

The war and its atrocities, especially the Holocaust, in which 6 million Jews were slaughtered, led to the founding of a new consciousness of human rights in Europe. Using the declaration as its model, the Council of Europe (the precursor of the European Union) adopted the European Convention on Human Rights in 1950 to protect human rights and political freedoms for all in Europe. The convention, today widely considered the most effective international treaty for human rights protections, also established the European Court of Human Rights, open to any person or group to seek redress for human rights violations.

Following the war, Germany amended its constitution to guarantee asylum for all victims of persecution. German Chancellor Angela Merkel called the Holocaust a "monumental shame" for her country and a "break with civilization." She has said, "The heart and soul of Europe is tolerance. It has taken us centuries to understand this. We have persecuted and annihilated one another. We have laid our country to waste. The worst period of hatred, devastation and destruction happened not even a generation ago. It was done in the name of my people." It was with this consciousness that Merkel and the German people welcomed over a million Syrian refugees in 2015.

Over half a million American Jews and 20,000 Canadian Jews served in the war and these returning veterans formed the backbone of the fight against entrenched anti-Semitism in both countries. Immigration policy was liberalized. Over 40,000 Holocaust survivors came to Canada in the 1940s and the US is now home to the largest Jewish diaspora in the world. It took decades for the last of the restrictions on Jews in universities and social clubs to end, but end they did.

Black American veterans returned from the war to lead the fight against white supremacy. They had fought and some of their brothers had died for their country, and they returned determined to assert their rights. Medgar Evers and his brother Charles, as well as other veterans, were among the first to demand the vote for Blacks in the South and became leaders in the NAACP and other Black justice organizations to end segregation. They were intensely aware that, at the same time their government was denouncing Hitler's ideas of Aryan supremacy, Black servicemen were treated like second-class citizens in the military and faced systemic racism and violence at home.

When the Student Nonviolent Coordinating Committee (SNCC) was formed in 1960, legendary leader Ella Baker made sure that older Black veterans formed a key nucleus in organizing voter registration in the Deep South.

Native Americans had the highest rate of voluntary enlistment in the Second World War. Of the 350,000 Native Americans at the time, 45,000 enlisted and another 65,000 went to work in the wartime defence industry. Yet it was not until November 11, 2020, with the opening of the Smithsonian's National Native American Veterans Memorial, that there was a landmark commemorating this contribution. Many Indigenous people in Canada fought with distinction as well, but it would be 50 years before they were allowed to lay a wreath on Remembrance Day. But those days did come.

Both Canada and the US initially opposed the 2007 United Nations Declaration on the Rights of Indigenous Peoples, a far-reaching resolution defining the individual and collective rights of Indigenous people around the world. But in 2010, President Barack Obama endorsed the resolution, and in 2016, Prime Minister Justin Trudeau followed suit.

In 1988, both Canada and the US formally apologized to people of Japanese descent for the internment camps their families suffered during the war. And in 2010, Canada formally apologized to the Indigenous victims of the residential school system.

These postwar years also saw the rise of a powerful labour movement. In many countries, workers gained an unprecedented measure of security against old age, illness and unemployment as well as a huge improvement in workplace rights. The rise of workers and labour unions paralleled the rise of social security for all and that was reflected in government legislation and international institutions. There were decades of strikes against unsafe working conditions and for better pay and benefits. Survivors of Canada's terrible 1919 strike in Winnipeg or the miners' strikes in Appalachia in the pre–First World War years must never have felt that things would get better, that change was not in their favour, and they would have been amazed and gratified at the workplace and social protections we now take for granted.

Before the Second World War in Canada, the notion of social security as a right of citizenship was almost non-existent. Aid was doled out as a form of charity in a patchwork of inadequate programs. But the war changed the nation. When Canadians went to war in 1939, the full force of the Canadian state went with them. The same government that did not have money to feed, clothe, employ or house people before the war suddenly had all the money it needed for a full-on war effort. Returning soldiers and their families were determined to build what my father, who served in the war for five years, called a "social nation state."

The consensus for change within Canadian society was broad and, within a decade, Canada had adopted universal old age security, family allowance and unemployment insurance. Within another decade, universal health insurance was the law of the land, guaranteeing all Canadians public health care regardless of income or social status.

There would, in time and inevitably, be a backlash to these programs and the role of the state in delivering social security. And it is clear with the rise of white supremacy movements and right-wing populism today that many individuals and institutions around the world never did buy in into this larger consensus. The point I want to make here, however, is that out of a great and terrible conflict came fundamental change in the way people viewed social and human rights. It led to the creation of a body of human rights law and obligations that had not existed before. The powerful movements of today for justice and equity stand on the shoulders of this legacy. Surely this is cause for hope. And a lesson for a post-COVID world.

Take hope from the goodness of others

I know that in progressive movements and activist organizations, competition, conflicts, disloyalty and even betrayal exist. We are human after all. But I choose not to linger on these encounters or experiences. I have been so unbelievably strengthened by the goodwill of others. I can hardly give enough credit to how it has helped me in my life's work. Dinner in the home of someone in a community you are visiting. Notes and letters and emails of support. A young student telling me she chose her field of study and career inspired by my work. A book of good wishes gathered by the staff of my organization wishing me all the best on my 50th, then 60th, then 70th birthday. I have kept them all.

Supportive friends, family and colleagues are the bed-rock of sanity for activists working with often heartbreaking struggles. It is imperative to support one another and to remind ourselves that we may not live to see the outcome of our work and that's okay. We can have great joy in the journey and one another. In an email to me, Vandana Shiva writes, "We owe each other a celebration of life and to replace fear and hopelessness with fearlessness and joy." I have had the privilege and luck of a wonderful supportive family, especially my husband, Andrew. And I have worked with the most amazing activists here in Canada and around the world. Their courage, good nature and sense of hope keeps me going.

British Columbian ecologist Suzanne Simard is credited with discovering the mycorrhizal fungal networks below the forest floor and the role they play in the life and health of trees and forests by carrying carbon and nitrogen through the ecosystem. A passionate defender of old-growth trees and forests, Simard says forests have much to teach humans. In a July 2021 interview with *The Narwhal*, she says forests have evolved to recover and regenerate, as have humans, with the help from a network of family and friends. "It is just that all these creatures are working at small scales and it builds and builds like a nucleus that's growing, and then the system can suddenly recover very quickly. . . . We have no choice but to remain hopeful, to continue to push and push and push as much as we possibly can in our own capacities and not exhaust ourselves." Simard advises us to surround ourselves with people who support us. "Then you can survive this."

When I think of instances where the goodness of others has helped me, many have involved strangers. I remember taking a bad fall on heaved pavement in Charleston, South Carolina, when I was there to speak at the university. A uniformed man who ran the local car park drove by and stopped to ask how I was. Fine, I said, not wanting to be a bother. He wasn't going to let it go at that. He circled around ten minutes later, and when he saw me still lying on the street, insisted on driving me to hospital.

I visited a community in rural Mexico and met with a group of women who were fighting for water justice and to have access to a local water pipe they could not afford. They lived in appalling conditions. No running water, no electricity, 12 people to a tin hut. But they insisted on bringing out their best water — rainwater collected with care in a cistern — to drink together, and we experienced moments of joy and delight when we shared it.

My luggage did not arrive with me when I embarked on a two-week book tour of Australia. Three women whom I had never met were there to greet me at the airport in Melbourne. They may as well have been friends for decades, so completely did we get along. When my suitcase arrived the next day, it had been soaked in some kind of awful chemical, my guess being de-icing fluid. The suitcase and everything in it was destroyed. My new friends went out and bought or gave me replacement clothes and necessities. I still have a treasured scarf from that visit. (Ever since, I never check my bags. I only bring carry-on, no matter how long the journey.)

I have no better example of the kindness of others than the stories of how complete strangers have reacted to what I can only refer to as my "intestinal issues." I had a strong constitution growing up but when I started to travel extensively about 30 years ago, I developed situational irritable bowel syndrome (IBS) and it has plagued me in my travels, leading to some mortifying experiences.

It began in 1990, when I attended an encuentro in Mexico City with a group of fellow Canadian labour and social justice activists for meetings with our Mexican counterparts in anticipation of the NAFTA negotiations our governments had started. After the Mexico City gathering, some of us went on a side tour of the maquiladoras (free trade factories) in and around Tijuana. We visited slums and factories and broke bread with many local people. Upon my return to Canada, my health problems started in earnest. I set out on a book tour for my first published book — *Parcel of Rogues*, on the Canada–US Free Trade Agreement — and I could barely survive a car ride, far less a plane ride. I had to warn interviewers that I might have to interrupt our chat for a bathroom emergency.

Anyone who has suffered from IBS understands. I have had to leave stages where I am to speak to find a bathroom. I have had accidents on streets and in cars. When I returned home for any length of time, things would normally settle down. But when I started to travel long distances again, my troubles would flare up. This was especially true of travels to the Global South, where, in spite of every precaution, I would drink some water or shake a hand or eat some food and that would be that.

Eventually I came to think of this ailment as my way of bringing the "Third World" to the "First World," for it is a scourge that afflicts so many in poor countries and in poor communities of rich countries. I promised myself I would spare the statistics in this book, but it bears repeating that over three billion people don't have a place to wash their hands with soap and warm water — the first thing we were told to do to combat COVID — and that over 1.5 million children die every year due to drinking dirty water. I came to have a closer understanding of these dry statistics with my own health issues originally contracted from contaminated water.

Everywhere I needed help, strangers were there for me, and I like to think I was there for them. One night, I was taken from my hotel to a Johannesburg hospital by ambulance with terrible intestinal cramps. Luckily I had travel insurance, so the hospital was one with excellent care. I had to stay for almost a week in pretty constant pain.

In the bed beside me was a young British woman who had been on her honeymoon touring several African countries. She and her new husband were in a boat on the Chobe River in Botswana when a hippopotamus charged their boat and hit it so hard, the young woman fell into the water. The hippo took her whole leg in its mouth, only letting go when her husband and the boat driver hit it repeatedly with oars. They airlifted her to Johannesburg where she almost died. By the time I met her, she had been in that hospital for seven months and was likely to be there at least another few before she could travel home. Her husband had left her, and she knew no one.

During the day she was busy with her therapy, but she quietly wept at night. I asked the nurse to move our beds closer together so I could reach out and hold her hand and we talked through many hours of pain. We kept in touch for a while after she returned to England and settled into a new life.

My trips to Latin America were especially hard on my health. I have come to love Bolivia. I have been there at least half a dozen times to support their fight to protect water and have visited remote communities and many urban slums. Every single time I came home ill. One trip is particularly memorable. I flew out of La Paz on American Airlines and, for some reason, was bumped up to first class. In the middle of the night, I rushed to the bathroom in real distress. I will spare you the details, gentle reader. Suffice to say I had to put all my clothes, including my shoes, in a plastic bag for disposal. A flight attendant with the unlikely but lovely name of Sky Blue gave me her black silk pyjamas and slippers to wear, else I would have had to stay in that bathroom.

When I arrived at my next destination, Calgary, I bought an adorable set of fleece polar bear pyjamas and matching slippers and sent them to Sky Blue with a note that said, "I was naked and ye clothed me."

How can I not be hopeful in a world that produced Sky Blue?

CHAPTER TWO

THE RISING OF THE WOMEN

We are the women men warned us about . . .
We are the women who will transform the world.

FROM "A WOMAN'S CREED"

My journey has taken me through three interrelated but distinct stages. My first work and love was for the women's movement within my own country. This caused me to question the dominant political narrative of the time and eventually led me to the international fight against economic globalization. During that work, I discovered the corporate assault on the world's water that was part of the globalization trend, and I turned my attention to the human right to water and sanitation. This brought me full circle, back to women, since finding water and caring for family is still primarily a woman's job in most parts of the world.

In this and the next two chapters, I will tell you more about these stages in my life and the lessons each taught me. All three were part of an enormous political and economic upheaval that would change the world. Each was fuelled by hope — sometimes just a blind hope — that the work we were doing would make a difference.

Growing up female in the mid-20th century

Like all women of my generation, I grew up with one foot in the old world for women and the other in the new.

In 1946 (the year before I was born), noted New York psychiatrist Dr. Ralph S. Banay, writing for *Colliers Magazine*, summed up what women of my mother's generation faced. He, and many other so-called experts, believed that women's emotional growth had not kept up with their intellectual and economic development and therefore they were closer to a childlike state of elemental nature than men. He wrote, "Women's total nature — conscious and subconscious — is comparable with that of preadolescent children and of men inclined to criminal propensities." And, he added, like all low offenders, women "crave mistreatment." This almost instinctual fascination with danger and horror were a "vestigial remembrance of the thrill and danger of the ancient hunts in which women were captured and subdued."

Yes, many women in 1950s and '60s Canada were entering the workforce and holding office. But a woman still could not open a bank account or apply for a passport without a male relative's signature; she could not testify against her husband for beating her or become ordained as a church minister. Most women had no legal access to birth control, and until 1988, abortion was difficult to access. Women teachers and civil servants had to hand in their resignations when they became pregnant. There was no maternity leave for women or unemployment insurance when they left the workforce. Many workplaces, including government offices at all levels, had separate pay levels for men and women right into the 1960s and even the 1970s in places. Pay gaps between the salaries of men and women were huge, resulting in poverty for many senior women living alone. Two-thirds of Canadians on welfare were women.

At school in Ottawa, I took home economics classes while the boys learned "shop" skills, mostly basic carpentry. We learned sewing, cooking and homemaking skills. In gym class, we wore baggy blue bloomers to hide our changing bodies. Sex education consisted of a film called *You're a Young Lady Now* that showed teenaged girls running through a meadow and made an obscure reference to a sanitary napkin with no indication of what that had to do with running. I belonged to the Canadian Girls in Training at my local United Church and, to my mortification now, we were taken in our middies at age 12 to a home for unwed mothers, where we stared at the poor girls who were serving as living cautionary tales.

It was expected that we would marry and have children and that any jobs we might have would be secondary to our husbands' careers. After all, we all had single female teachers who had had to choose between marriage and their teaching jobs when the men returned from war. We pitied their spinster lives and made up terrible stories to explain their lack of husbands.

But I had been raised at home to name and fight injustice, so when I opened my eyes to the discrimination against women surrounding me as water surrounds fish, it hit hard. I was a young mother with small children when the full brunt of the modern women's movement hit in the late 1960s and '70s, and I jumped into the deep end of the pool. I started reading everything I could get my hands on: Virginia Woolf, Simone de Beauvoir, Germaine Greer, Betty Friedan, Robin Morgan, Gloria Steinem.

American feminist scholar Andrea Dworkin was my turning point. She wrote *Woman Hating*, an anthology of religious and state oppression of women throughout the ages. In the mid-1970s, I heard her give one of her impassioned speeches, this one in Toronto, and it was a call to arms for me. She thundered from the pulpit like an old-time gospel preacher, explaining how she became a feminist. She had been working with the civil rights movement in the Deep South in the 1960s, when a Black activist colleague disappeared. They dragged a local swamp for his body and found lots of bodies, the searchers said, but not him. Just a bunch of women, Black and white, probably prostitutes, nothing to get worried about. Dworkin said that the men who dismissed these dead women were not local rednecks, but compatriots in the civil rights struggle. Her anger at this event fuelled her pioneering work.

Writing about this story now puts me in mind of today's Canadian campaign to face the tragedy of missing and murdered Indigenous women and girls. Being Indigenous rendered them invisible to both the justice system and the mainstream Canadian populace and it would be decades before Canadian society would recognize this.

I join the most exciting movement of my time

It was exhilarating, the combination of rage, joy, excitement and hope that fuelled this stage of the fight for women's equality. We believed it was a new day and nothing was going to stop us. The first lesson I learned from these years was that governments and other major institutions were not going to give rights and power away. They remained wedded to the status quo and it was up to us to organize and fight for our rights. The suffragettes and other early feminists had worked hard and sacrificed much for the right to vote and to have legal personhood and to own property. (The pre-1917 Elections Act of the Dominion of Canada stated, "No woman, idiot, lunatic or child shall vote.") But there was much more still to be done and we knew we would have to organize if we were to take up the challenge.

The first lesson I learned from these years was that governments and other major institutions were not going to give rights and power away . . . and it was up to us to organize and fight for our rights.

Dozens of women's groups were formed at this time and one common demand in Canada was for a royal commission to investigate and to compile a report on the systemic discrimination women faced. The Royal Commission on the Status of Women was launched in 1967. Its report three years later changed the world for Canadian women. Its 167 recommendations touched on everything from employment rights, equal pay, maternity leave and pensions to educational opportunities. Women's groups were quick to put huge pressure on governments to act on the report.

Governments started funding rape crisis centres, career counselling services and transition houses for battered women, as they were called at the time. The federal government mandated training programs for women in the workplace and established the Canadian Advisory Council on the Status of Women and Status of Women Canada, adopted the Canadian Human Rights Act and amended the Canada Labour Code to remove discriminatory statutes and practices everywhere. After a fierce national protest, the rights of women were enshrined in the 1982 Charter of Rights and Freedoms, which basically assures that any law that is inconsistent with the charter is invalid. Three years later, Indigenous women won full status in the charter as well.

There were no women's studies or human rights courses in universities at the time, and so many of us forged careers in the advancement of women from what we learned volunteering and at gatherings where we shared our experiences (called consciousness raising) and with sheer innovation. I volunteered in a number of ways, including at a women's addiction centre and a women's shelter, and studied women's equality training courses from women who were creating them in the UK and the US. I also monitored and charted the negative images of women in the media, gave presentations in schools and universities and appeared before several commissions on violence against women in the media, all as a volunteer.

In 1975, with several other women, I formed Women Associates Consulting Incorporated, a consulting group to advance the status of women in all facets of Canadian society. We were the first of our kind in Canada but our company was modelled on several American organizations that were blazing a trail armed with mandated Affirmative Action legislation. Without such legislation in Canada, we had to use the power of persuasion with Canadian employers. We were not above reminding them that if they didn't take action to improve working conditions for women in their workforce, the government would be forced to introduce laws similar to those in the US.

We had an incredible five years of providing advice, research and training nationally on how to further women's rights and promote women in organizations and businesses. We designed assertiveness and management training and career counselling for women. And we designed pay-equity and gender-based workforce planning programs and sensitivity training for managers. Among our contracts were the Alberta Human Rights Commission, the National Indian Brotherhood (predecessor of the Assembly of First Nations), Atomic Energy of Canada, the Canadian Police College, Ontario Hydro, the National Film Board and the CBC, where we put every manager and more than 1,000 women through equal-opportunity training. I remember one diehard senior manager at the CBC telling me that he could tell which women had taken my course: "They talk back!"

What struck me then — and still — is how many women internalize negative stereotypes about themselves and hold low opinions of their own capabilities. This is the second lesson I learned in my years with the women's movement. We had been raised to take our "proper" place in society, and we were taught to judge ourselves and one another on appearance and a standard ideal of beauty. We were raised to be people pleasers, to seek approval and bury our gifts and ambitions. It was hard for us to assert our rights for fear we would offend; our need for approval could be incapacitating. (This was also an issue of survival: there was the very real fact that many were dependent on male bosses who did not want to be questioned.) Even women who seemed self-assured and successful often suffered from imposter syndrome, a belief that they were not deserving of their success. This phenomenon is still prevalent among women and other groups underrepresented due to their class or race.

I learned that centuries of conditioning had taught women to protect themselves by being nice and not causing trouble but, of course, it held us back. I had the same tug of war inside me. As the middle child of three girls, I got my way by being a peacemaker. But I also had strong opinions and a tendency to express them. I will always remember the first time I was publicly criticized and feeling sorry for myself. My wise mother told me to cut it out, that this came with the territory I had chosen, and reminded me that "serious people have serious enemies."

I realized we had to help one another undo these centuries of oppression and internalized behaviour. In our sessions, my colleagues and I taught women (and ourselves) that they are allowed to act in their own self-interest, to ask for what they need, to set limits on other people's aggression and to express negative feelings. Many a session ended with each woman finishing the statement "I like myself because . . ." It was a hard and liberating exercise for every woman who went through our programs. I bet it still would be today.

Fighting for women in the strangest places

My career in the women's movement took me to places where women had it the roughest and taught me a great deal about hope. I was the first woman to teach at the Canadian Police College, a national training school for police managers across the country. Violence against women was a huge social issue and police badly needed training to deal with its victims. Wife assault was considered a private matter and many a police officer had walked a husband around the block to "cool off" after an "incident." I worked with women in rape crisis centres who told of rape victims being interviewed in rooms at the police station whose walls were plastered with photos of nude women. It was my job to impart to the police at the college the emerging societal and government consensus that these were crimes, not family feuds, and needed to be treated as such.

In 1977, I became involved in the fight to open up the armed services to women and I helped design the pilot assessment for women in near-combat roles at the military training centre in Saint-Jean, Quebec. When the trials were done, senior management at the Department of Defence wrote an internal report indicating that, even though women had done well on the trials, they were going to advise against allowing women into combat or near-combat roles as men were having a hard time adapting to their presence. The report was leaked to me in a brown paper bag, and I got it on the front page of the *Globe and Mail* the next day. National media followed this story avidly and the department had to get busy defending itself.

In 1985, our new group, the Association for Women's Equity in the Canadian Forces, appeared before the parliamentary subcommittee on equality rights and presented a brief with a series of recommendations that were unanimously approved and later backed by the results of a Human Rights Tribunal ruling. Most occupations in the Canadian armed forces were opened to women within a few years; the last restriction, serving on submarines, ended in 2000.

These inroads into such occupations as the armed forces and policing were significant and the law was with women. But this is one of the hard lessons learned. Gaining rights in court or Parliament is a vital part of the job, but making the victories real can take a long time — hence the need to not link success solely to one outcome. Advancement comes in stages and is usually met with renewed resistance from those who see their power diminished.

To this day, women face harassment in these and other male-dominated workplaces in spite of laws affirming their equal rights. In November 2019, the Federal Court of Canada approved a $900-million class-action settlement for survivors of sexual harassment and assault in the military and, a year later, certified a $1.1-billion class-action claim against the RCMP for condoning an environment of systemic bullying, intimidation and sexual harassment and for fostering a toxic workplace. It is clear that the more militaristic the work environment, the less comfortable it is for women. If ever these institutions, such as policing, are going to change in response to widespread public criticisms of a culture of aggression and violence, they will need to truly welcome, not just tolerate, women and other underrepresented groups.

> *Advancement comes in stages and is usually met with renewed resistance from those who see their power diminished.*

I also worked at the other end of the law-enforcement system, with the infamous, now closed Prison for Women, P4W. Built in 1934, and little changed until the day it closed, it was situated just down the road from the men's prison in Kingston. An ugly, dark, imposing grey cement monster, it housed all the federal female offenders in Canada in conditions from a time when incarceration was meant to be a brutal and punitive experience. As part of my work with Women Associates, I was brought in to give anger-management and life skills workshops to the inmates of

P4W for three years, starting in 1978. Inside was a collection of the most disadvantaged and dispossessed people I had ever met being handled by overworked, understaffed and, in some cases, aggressive guards, many of whom were men.

It was my experience that most incarcerated women have histories of poverty, sexual violence, incest, racism and brutality, and most have internalized a terrible sense of self-hatred. My time at P4W offered some of the most intense personal interactions of my life and I learned so much from those incarcerated women. They had formed a rough form of sisterhood necessary to survival. My task was to work with them to see their "crimes" against the larger backdrop of the systemic discrimination that existed in society, especially for women of colour and Indigenous women, who were — and still are — overrepresented in Canadian jails.

There were women who had murdered violent partners, and women who were alcoholics or drug addicts who had not been conscious enough to protect their children from a blazing fire or a nearby lake. There were women who ran drugs for men who beat them, and sex workers who hurt men in self-defence. Several women would mutilate their bodies with razors and other hidden objects. One woman was halfway through gender confirmation surgery and had been moved from the men's prison down the road. As we sat in a musty, old, barely furnished room, bars on the tiny high windows, with armed guards pacing outside, one by one, the women of P4W told their stories of survival and their dreams of a future outside those walls. There, I learned the meaning of hope.

The discrimination they endured was blatant. Women at P4W received less counselling for alcohol and drug abuse than the inmates of the men's prison They had limited training compared to the men, and the little they had was in traditionally female occupations such as hair dressing. They were even given less money for transportation and shelter than the men when they left prison. One guard told me it was because it was assumed they would sell sex to make money. Because there was only one federal prison, women were all housed as maximum offenders, even if they were classified as minimum, and most were far from home and cut off from their families and cultures.

One by one, the women of P4W told their stories of survival and their dreams of a future outside those walls. There, I learned the meaning of hope.

Outraged at this injustice, I joined a number of women in the criminal justice field (including my criminologist sister Christine Jefferson) to fight for the rights of the women at P4W. Calling ourselves Women for Justice, we launched a landmark case with the Canadian Human Rights Commission against the Canadian Penitentiary Service. In December 1981, the commission ruled that the women at P4W were victims of discrimination and ordered the beginning of a process to close the prison down. The first women were transferred to new and better provincial facilities in 1994 and P4W was finally closed in 2000. Importantly, the commission found that the Correctional Service of Canada, as a whole, was practising systemic discrimination and mandated an overhaul, including training and pay equity.

To thank us, a group of P4W inmates serving life sentences invited our group to a celebration and concert at the prison. They called it "Career Day for Lifers." Now that's hope.

Fighting for women at city hall

The City of Ottawa in the 1970s and '80s was like most municipal governments in Canada — notorious for its paternalistic hiring and employment practices. There was no human resources manual, no hiring or employment procedures and no job interview panels. Managers, supervisors and foremen hired friends and family — no questions asked. Women made up only 22% of the workforce and the pay gap was so large that a man with a grade eight education made more money than a woman with a university degree.

In 1980, I was hired to be the director of the Office of Equal Opportunity for Women for the City of Ottawa. There was only one other such office in Canada, in Vancouver, and no blueprint to follow. I had to make everything up as I went along. I was getting used to this, for I found myself the first at many things I tackled. This was another lesson I learned early on in my activism: Don't wait for a path to be laid out in detail, with instructions and a map. Jump in and do your best with instinct, good intentions, common sense and hope as your guides.

At city hall, I was greeted with a great deal of suspicion and even hostility by some of the managers, all but one of whom were men. But I reported directly to the mayor, the wonderful Marion Dewar, and to her council, which had a surprising number of female councillors (a direct result of a strong local women's movement), and from them, I received enormous support. Working with the personnel department, my colleague Bonnie Diamond and I designed a human resources manual requiring fairer hiring and employment practices. We designed a pilot program on job sharing and issued a feasibility study on a city hall day-care centre. We implemented one of the first municipal bylaws in the country to deal with workplace sexual harassment and developed career and life skills training programs for female employees.

Don't wait for a path to be laid out in detail, with instructions and a map. Jump in and do your best with instinct, good intentions, common sense and hope as your guides.

One of our most controversial projects was hiring women as labourers, arena attendants, snow-clearing and heavy equipment operators, groundskeepers, asphalt repair workers and sewer maintenance workers — all blue-collar jobs traditionally done by men. Hundreds of women applied, and we hired the first group who were watched like rats in a maze by other staff, city councillors, the local media and, most of all, their male co-workers. They were put through tests that their male counterparts had not endured, but they could live with that, they told me. What most could not endure were the threats of violence for entering a male space and most of the early hires left.

This was a period of heightened concern about violence against women. Violent and sexist ads for movies in my local newspaper when my kids were young first alerted me to the connection between how women are depicted in the media and how they are treated in the home and the workplace. I served on MediaWatch, then a national women's organization that monitored the portrayal of women in the media, and in 1976 appeared before the Ontario Royal Commission on Violence in the Communications Industry, chaired by the fiery Judy LaMarsh. At the City of Ottawa, I brought in guidelines for the depiction of women in ads on city buses and property.

When, in early 1983, First Choice, the first licensed pay TV channel in Canada, announced a contract with Playboy, women across the country held rallies and boycotted Eaton's, the parent company of First Choice, to national headlines. The issue was hotly debated in the House of Commons, and in the end, the company backed off. The controversy launched heavy debate about sexism and violence in mainstream pornography and set the stage for a parliamentary study of pornography and prostitution, not from a position of public morality but as a question of the human rights of the women in the sex trade.

Attitudes toward violence against women were hard to change. In a 1996 column for *Maclean's*, journalist Barbara Amiel wrote that wife assault was "domestic strife between consenting adults," and that "some people have a psycho-sexual orientation that requires pain for full satisfaction." A 1982 House of Commons report on battered women was met with guffaws of laugher from male MPs, causing waves of anger from women's groups across Canada.

I was proud to set up the Ottawa Task Force on Wife Assault the next year, one of the first in Canada. We brought together family services, women's shelters, the police, the hospitals, the Crown Attorney's office, defence lawyers and the board of education. While the task force studied all the newest research and statistics on wife assault, what really brought us together were the testimonies of the battered women who appeared before us as part of our public outreach. Their stories changed hearts and minds in a way that no set of statistics ever could.

One woman, a mother of six, lived on a farm in a remote part of the Ottawa Valley. Her husband became increasingly possessive over the years, not allowing her to see family, friends or neighbours and eventually chaining her to her bed, where he fed her only sporadically and beat her regularly. She only escaped when her adult children held a rescue mission and took her to a shelter. She told our committee that if he found her, he would kill her. This kind of testimony changed minds and the task force came together to fight for her and the other women who were brave enough to speak to us.

Our report to city council was well received and established a new municipal protocol for dealing with family violence. It morphed into an implementation committee that coordinated family violence response in Ottawa for years. Another lesson learned: go to the heart of the human story to touch hearts as well as minds if you want to get people out of their silos.

Fighting for women in the highest place

All the political parties were keenly aware of what was newly called the "gender gap," the fact that women often had different views from men on many issues, ranging from childcare to war. These views affected how women voted, and the gender gap was showing up in polling. Newspaper headlines declared, "Politicians are learning the peril of ignoring women" and "Gender gap gives women clout at the polls." The political parties all took note and started courting the women's vote big time.

In the summer of 1983, I was appointed senior advisor on women to then prime minister Pierre Elliot Trudeau — a new position. I thought long and hard about taking this position. I was not a Liberal, but I was not particularly partisan anyway, preferring to do my work outside mainstream politics. It was common knowledge that Trudeau was tired of politics and might not lead the party into the next election. However, if he were to stay, a major focus of the platform would be women's equality issues, and I was to write up the blueprint for their agenda. It was a gamble I took to be able to advance women's rights from the highest office in the land. In the end, of course, Trudeau took his famous walk in the snow in February 1984, and his departure became my own.

But there are two initiatives I worked on for the short time I was there that were meaningful to me and gave me great hope. The first was the fight for gender equality of First Nations women. Under the 1867 Indian Act, an "Indian" was defined as male and the bloodline was passed through the male lineage. Status Indian women lost their status rights if they married a non-status or non-Indigenous man, whereas that was not the case for status men marrying non-status women. This glaring discriminatory provision led to the loss of on-reserve property rights and the assimilation and disenfranchisement of Indigenous women and their children. It also institutionalized male privilege within First Nations band councils.

Mary Two-Axe Earley was a champion for the rights of Indigenous women and became a friend and mentor to me that year. A Mohawk from Kahnawà:ke, she had lost her status when she married off-reserve. This led her to form the groups Indian Rights for Indian Women in 1967 and the Quebec Native Women's Association in 1974. I worked in the background to get political support inside the PMO for Two-Axe Earley and the Native Women's Association of Canada in their fight for an amendment to remove gender discrimination in the Indian Act to bring it in line with the Charter of Rights and Freedoms. Their campaign was finally successful in 1985, and Mary Two-Axe Earley regained her status and moved back to her community just before she died at age 84.

The other project that captured my heart and imagination was Pierre Trudeau's Peace Initiative, launched just after I started working for him. The early 1980s was a time of great tension among the superpowers and nuclear weapons were being steadily stockpiled around the world. Ronald Reagan was in the White House, heating up the Cold War rhetoric, and massive anti-war demonstrations were taking place across Europe. Trudeau set out on a whirlwind tour of other countries to try to de-escalate global tensions. His goals were to host the five major nuclear powers at a conference to stabilize and hopefully reduce their weapons stockpiles, to cut conventional forces in Europe and to strengthen the 1968 Nuclear Non-proliferation Treaty.

While many Canadians were skeptical of this project, seeing it as an attempt by the Liberals to boost their sagging fortunes, I saw up close that this was a project dear to Trudeau's heart. Perhaps he saw it as a legacy issue. While he and his foreign affairs officials were organizing internationally, I was reaching out to Canadian women's peace groups and advocates for advice and support. Luckily for me, this effort put me in touch with the great Canadian author Margaret Laurence, who was supportive of the Trudeau peace initiative and with whom I formed a close bond in the years until her death in 1987.

Try to feel, in your heart's core, the reality of others. This is the most painful thing in the world, probably, and the most necessary.

— MARGARET LAURENCE

Laurence was deeply affected by the buildup of nuclear weapons. In a speech to Trent University in March 1983 called "My Final Hour," she shared her fear about a future in which there would be no succeeding generations, in which all the works of the human imagination would be destroyed, never to be seen or listened to or experienced again. And yet Laurence gave her audience of young people a vision of hope and this advice: "Try to feel, in your heart's core, the reality of others. This is the most painful thing in the world, probably, and the most necessary. In times of personal adversity, know that you are not alone. Know that, although in the eternal scheme of things you are small, you are also unique and irreplaceable, as are all of your fellow humans everywhere in the world. Know that your commitment is above all to life itself."

Lessons from the trenches

My commitment to the women's movement would never be done, but this phase of my career was coming to an end. I had learned so much during these turbulent years and I knew these lessons would serve me well going forward.

So what did I learn? I have mentioned several things already.

1. Governments and other powerful institutions are not going to give up power without a fight. Rights have to be fought for and taken.
2. Oppressed peoples often internalize negative stereotypes about themselves and have to consciously reject them and support one another in creating new self-narratives.
3. Gaining rights through a new law or court case, or a human rights or charter challenge, does not end the struggle. In many cases, it has just begun, and there will almost certainly be a backlash.
4. Don't wait for a path to be well trodden before you set out on it. You can be the one to walk it first.

5. Go to the heart of the human story if you want to break down silos and come together in common cause.

The women's movement changed society

These years of change revealed that confronting patriarchy changed much more than the role of women in society. While the goal of some feminists of my generation was strict equality for women inside the system, many of us were clear that we were going to use our new-found influence to challenge and change the system itself.

It was never my personal goal to gain strict 50% equality with men, as I was critical of some of the foundations upon which they had built our society.

It was never my personal goal to gain strict 50% equality with men, as I was critical of some of the foundations upon which they had built our society.

In 1970, American feminist icon Gloria Steinem wrote an essay for *TIME* called "What It Would Be Like If Women Win," in which she clearly stated that women don't want to exchange places with men. Men who interpreted the women's movement in that way did so based on ruling-class ego and guilt, she wrote. Steinem foresaw the ways in which the gender and race struggles would influence one another. "Men assume that women want to imitate them, which is just what white people assumed about blacks. An assumption so strong that it may convince the second-class groups of the need to imitate, but for both women and blacks that stage has passed.

Guilt produces the question: What if they could treat us as we have treated them?"

That same year, Robin Morgan, another American feminist, edited a collection called *Sisterhood Is Powerful*, in which she echoed these thoughts. "But we no longer feel foolish," she wrote in the foreword. "We have learned to take ourselves seriously and that is very far to have come. We rejoice that we are struggling together. We mark our progress in grains of sand heaped against the tide: a senator here, an executive there, a center for displaced homemakers, a sympathetic newspaper editorial, a construction job. We can take courage (whistling in the backlash darkness) from the opposition, because they have taken us more seriously than we have ourselves. They knew before we did that such apparently simple ideas as equal pay, equal rights, and equal parenting mean in fact redistribution of wealth, reallocation of power, and redefinition of roles."

> We can take courage (whistling in the backlash darkness) from the opposition, because they have taken us more seriously than we have ourselves.
>
> — ROBIN MORGAN

Morgan went on to say that every woman who accepts her new opportunity without opening the door for other women to change the system stands with the tide. "For the point of feminism is not that the world should be the same, but that it should be different."

In fact, what women of my generation learned from this struggle would stand us in good stead as we branched out into other areas of concern, from the anti-nuclear movement to the environment. We could bring a feminist view and another dimension of thought to these new efforts. A prime example is ecofeminism, a movement and philosophy that sees critical connections between the domination of nature and the exploitation of women and minorities.

As Vandana Shiva explained in her 2014 anthology *Ecofeminism*, feminists learned that science and technology are not gender neutral and are often used to uphold a system that oppresses both nature and women. "The capitalist-patriarchal perspective interprets difference as hierarchical and uniformity as a prerequisite for equality. Our aim is to go beyond this narrow perspective and to express our diversity and, in different ways, address the inherent inequalities in world structures which permit the North to dominate the South, men to dominate women, and the frenetic plunder of ever more resources for ever more unequally distributed economic gain to dominate nature."

The work is never done, but that's okay

I have watched people give up on a cause for which they have been fighting, often just before they are about to succeed. It takes a long time to change public opinion but, when it happens, change in policy can come quickly. When I was growing up, drinking and driving was something cool guys bragged about. Not anymore. Smoking wherever you wanted regardless of others was accepted. Not anymore. But sometimes it is hard to visualize success when it still looks so far away. In fact, in my experience, as we come closer to achieving our goals, the resistance grows stronger and it may seem like we will never win.

The fight for childcare in Canada is a great example of women who would not give up their fight for a just and universal system. A safe, publicly funded, universal childcare system has been the goal of the women's movement in Canada for decades. According to Child Care Now, in 2021, there are enough licensed childcare spaces for only one in four Canadian children under six and many families struggle to pay for unregulated alternatives. A national childcare advocacy coalition was formed at a conference in 1982, but it wasn't until fall 2020 that the federal government finally announced its plans for a national system.

It takes a long time to change public opinion but, when it happens, change in policy can come quickly.

This "work is never done" lesson is related to my earlier one that winning a goal, such as a new law or legal challenge, does not end the struggle. On the contrary, it is often the start of a whole new phase of the work. I have written of the sexual and personal harassment women endure after having won the right to move into male preserves such as policing and the military. But the whole #MeToo movement is really the next iteration of the ongoing fight for equality and dignity for women, the logical extension of the gains made in the last decades. As women become more powerful, the threats against them often increase. While male politicians get trolled, successful women politicians are targets of terrible abuse, from comments on their appearance to threats of violence and assault.

Ellen Gabriel

Ellen Gabriel is a Mohawk activist and artist from Kanehsata:ke Nation, Turtle Clan. She was chosen by the People of the Longhouse to be the official spokesperson during the Oka Crisis of 1990. In speaking about the pain of the Oka confrontation, Gabriel once said that just knowing that it might have helped one small First Nations community to be empowered made it worthwhile.

Where do you find hope?

"Growing up in Kanehsata:ke, I was privileged to be able to play on the land: to feel the smell of all its beauty and wonders

"my family are traditionally farmers and have always worked the land so they taught me how important and precious land is

"so what gives me hope is to protect the land for present and future generations to cherish and enjoy

"to know what it is like to be in the forest, with trees we fought

"to protect in 1990

"and in knowing the long history of Resistance which the Kanien'kehà:ka peoples have in protecting the land.

"Our ancestral teachings centre around respect and honouring the lands and all our relations

"Mother Earth nourishes us, and when we are troubled, she creates the winds, the quietness and peace of the Land

"To bring us back to our good minds

"knowing this brings me HOPE."

Abuse against women journalists is also rampant. A November 2020 global survey of women journalists conducted by the International Center for Journalists found that three-quarters of survey participants said they have experienced online abuse, harassment, threats and attacks. Twenty percent also reported offline abuse and attacks that they believe were connected to the online violence they had experienced. The risk extends to the families of women journalists, including threats to their children, leading the women to keep a low profile on social media.

And, of course, there is the reality that a right won can be challenged. Those who would deny women reproductive rights were thrilled when former president Donald Trump appointed Amy Coney Barrett to the US Supreme Court. She has written that abortion is "always immoral" in the eyes of her church and, in early September 2021, sided with other conservative Supreme Court justices in refusing to block a Texas law that amounts to a ban on abortions after six weeks of pregnancy.

Winning a goal, such as a new law or legal challenge, does not end the struggle. On the contrary, it is often the start of a whole new phase of the work.

As well, our understanding of an issue changes as we learn more. Back when we were fighting familial violence against women in the 1970s and '80s, there was strong agreement within the women's movement that there should be mandatory charging of men in a domestic violence or sexual assault incident. We called for police to consider assault by a partner the same as assault by a stranger. Today people call for society to punish men who sexually abuse women, and the penalties range from the death penalty for rapists in India to hefty fines for men who verbally harass women on the street in France, to Hollywood, where there is little sympathy for the incarceration of celebrities such as Harvey Weinstein and Bill Cosby. But now there are other feminists who say that using police and prisons to deal with sexual violence doesn't work and that relying on state authority to curb domestic violence harms marginalized women. They challenge carceral feminists to understand that using the police and the law to deal with violence ignores the way class, race, gender identity and immigration status leave certain women more vulnerable to state violence and endanger their male partners inside prison.

Our understanding of an issue changes as we learn more.

Bonnie Diamond has had a distinguished career fighting for women as executive director of organizations such as the Canadian Association of Elizabeth Fry Societies and the National Association of Women and the Law. She says her early views of how to deal with male abusers were challenged when she was with the Canadian Panel on Violence Against Women in the early 1990s and heard how Indigenous women, for instance, were treated in the system when they called the police. She agrees that the system is biased against poor women and women of colour and wants more limited use of police and more services by people trained to deal with conflict. "We really have to reimagine crime and punishment. We have to look at the roots of crime and invest in encouraging the growth of healthy humans, getting rid of the blighting early so that most grow strong and can live peacefully in a more equal society," said Diamond in an email to me. "We also have to do early intervention with people whose needs were not met as children or young adults or who are on the streets." She admits this will require investment but points out that locking people up is also expensive.

The point I am trying to make here — and the lesson I learned — is that the struggle for justice is ongoing and never over. We can and do make real progress, but there are always new challenges or old challenges dressed up in the colours of the present. The joy is in the struggle. Or as Gandhi said, "The path is the goal." And as we travel this path, we make change upon which others build. Therein lies hope.

The joy is in the struggle.

Embracing diversity is crucial to moving forward

Perhaps the last big lesson I learned in these years was about my white privilege. My family was not wealthy. My father had a social worker's income, and my mother did not work outside the home and sewed most of my clothes, so I never thought of myself as privileged. I grew up in a white neighbourhood and went to schools and churches that were overwhelming white. News anchors were white. Movie stars were mostly white. White people dominated television and advertising. It took me years of working outside this "white zone" to begin to understand the reality of others who were not white or middle class.

A recurring criticism of the women's movement of the 1960s to the 1990s, often called second-wave feminism, is that it was led by and advanced the interests of white women — often women of privilege. There is much truth to this critique. When I look back on the task forces and royal commissions and parliamentary hearings of the time, they were almost always led by white feminist leaders. The Royal Commission on the Status of Women had no Indigenous women or women of colour as commissioners. The movement was largely based on the cultural and historical experiences of middle- and upper-class heterosexual white women. As American history scholar Arica L. Coleman explained in a March 2019 *TIME* article, consideration of race, class, sexuality, immigration and ableism was largely missing.

Many of the victories we had and the changes we made such as pay equity and reproductive rights benefitted all women regardless of their race or class — in theory. In reality, I soon learned that a privileged white urban woman had access to abortion clinics not available to poor rural women or Indigenous women living on reserve. And a white female lawyer or government official was aiming to match her salary to that of a well-paid male colleague, whereas a woman cleaning other people's houses or working as a dishwasher in an unregulated long-term care facility struggled to survive.

Black and other non-white feminist scholars developed theoretical frameworks that broadened feminism's definition and scope, reports Coleman. Many have been working for a more expansive and inclusive definition of feminism, one that recognizes the different realities faced by women of colour, Black women, LGBTQ+ women and

Indigenous women. Intersectionality is an understanding that all women do not share the same level of discrimination just because they are women. When the mainstream is prejudiced against other aspects of their identities, women cope with multiple, compounding forms of discrimination that must inform feminist work. Intersectionality is an essential part of the message from the Black Lives Matter and Idle No More movements — the latter founded in Canada by Indigenous women.

Gloria Steinem says the #MeToo movement has a blind spot when it comes to recognizing the essential role that Black women have played in the fight against sexual harassment. In a December 2017 interview with *Quartz Magazine*, she said Black women were early pioneers in filing successful sexual harassment lawsuits and that the #MeToo movement was launched by Tarana Burke, a Black woman. Steinem points to polls that show much higher support for feminist issues among Black women than white women back in the 1970s when she was launching *Ms. Magazine.* She also points out that Black women voted overwhelmingly for Hillary Clinton in the 2016 presidential election, while a majority of white women voted for Donald Trump.

The only way to build a healthy women's movement is to honour the perspectives of diverse women. Says Steinem, "We are not born sexist or racist. Rather, systemic racism and misogyny socializes us to believe that we are ranked, when in fact we are linked."

And of course, the situation for women in many parts of the world is not the same as it is in North America and

Europe. In its 2019–20 report on the status of women globally, the UN noted many advances for women but added that there were still huge hurdles. Three billion women and girls live in countries where rape within marriage is not explicitly criminalized. In one in five countries, girls do not have the same inheritance rights as boys, and in 19 countries, women are required by law to obey their husbands. One-third of married women in the Global South report having little or no say over their own health care.

The only way to build a healthy women's movement is to honour the perspectives of diverse women.

And a January 2020 report by the World Economic Forum said it will take another 257 years for women to reach pay equity with men around the world. The voices of women from the Global South are crucial to a more just and fair world.

As women face the future, we are stronger if we are inclusive and diverse. Movements must be constantly renewed and revitalized with new voices, new perspectives and new visions of hope. This is another important lesson.

The Women's Environment & Development Organization is an international movement that advocates for women's equality in global policy and has had a powerful impact on many UN documents and resolutions. It works to advance women's perspectives in policy areas such as peace, the climate crisis, biodiversity and conflict. At a gathering in New York City in 1994, the organization wrote "A Woman's Creed," a statement of rights and dreams that transcend differences and speaks for all women everywhere: "Bread. A clean sky. Active peace.

A woman's voice singing somewhere, melody drifting like smoke from the cook-fires. The army disbanded, the harvest abundant. The wound healed, the child wanted, the prisoner freed, the body's integrity honored, the lover returned. The magical skill that reads marks into meaning. The labor equal, fair and valued. Delight in the challenge for consensus to solve problems. No hand raised in any gesture but greeting. Secure interiors — of heart, home, land — so firm as to make secure borders irrelevant at last. And everywhere laughter, care, celebrations, dancing, contentment. A humble, earthly paradise, in the now."

Movements must be constantly renewed and revitalized with new voices, new perspectives and new visions of hope.

CHAPTER THREE

CHALLENGING CORPORATE RULE

The longing for a better world will need to arise at the imagined meeting place of many movements of resistance, as many as there are sites of closure and exclusion. The resistance will be as transnational as capital.

IAIN BOAL, "UP FROM THE BOTTOM,"

FIRST WORLD, HA, HA, HA!

My years in the women's movement taught me to question authority — all authority. I also learned to recognize how the powerful create institutions, networks and political structures that protect their interests. This in turn led me to question the economic and political narrative circulating in rarefied circles in the 1980s that would lead to economic globalization.

I began to realize that I needed to understand the promises being made by the institutions of the "new economy" that emerged right around the time women were making such inroads in the old one, and that it was imperative to challenge how they were affecting the rights of people all over the world. This would be a journey that began locally, fighting a free trade deal in order to protect Canadian social programs, many of which aided women, and progressed to the international stage, where I became part of a movement fighting the very structures of economic globalization, chasing its architects wherever they met, from Seattle to Cancun to Hong Kong.

I came to believe deeply — and do now more than ever — that when governments sign over sovereign rights to protect their people, culture and resources to the market as they do in a free trade agreement, the work of those fighting for social and environmental justice is profoundly impacted. If activists don't know about these forces of economic globalization, they are working with one arm tied behind their backs.

One cannot be politically and economically literate without being knowledgeable about how free trade, deregulation and privatization — the cornerstones of economic globalization often deliberated in faraway boardrooms or over dinners in elegant restaurants — are making our work so much more difficult. This is a lesson that took me years to understand, and I worry that it has been lost to a new generation of activists who think the fight about economic globalization and free trade is over.

I soon found out that where I was very much swimming *with* the tide of a movement whose time had come when I was fighting for justice for women, I would be swimming *against* the tide in fighting the powerful market forces that shaped the later decades of the 20th century. I learned that it is easier to be hopeful when you are on the winning side of history, but it is more important to be hopeful when you seem to be fighting the tide every step of the way.

The backlash against democracy

The postwar government social and rehabilitation programs helped create a middle class with money to spend that led to decades of prosperity in Europe and North America. But like any advancement, they created a backlash. By the late 1970s, many voices in government and the private sector were calling for a reduced role for government and an increased one for the market and the private companies within it. Social security programs had created an "excess of democracy," according to a 1975 report by the Trilateral Commission, an association of influential individuals formed in 1973 to encourage closer economic cooperation between Japan, western Europe and North America. At the same time, other powerful voices were calling for the "reform" of key international institutions that had been set up after the war.

It is easier to be hopeful when you are on the winning side of history, but it is more important to be hopeful when you seem to be fighting the tide every step of the way.

These institutions had been created at a July 1944 gathering of delegates from 44 allied nations in the small New Hampshire town of Bretton Woods, many of whom signed a far-reaching postwar agreement to promote peace and rebuild the international economic system. The World Bank was originally established to oversee the reconstruction of western Europe, and the International

Monetary Fund (IMF) was created to promote currency stability and global economic growth and prosperity. Both included a commitment to foster domestic policies that promoted full employment and accepted the rights of nations to regulate in the interests of their citizens.

Most notably, the Bretton Woods agreement was founded on the belief that, if further wars were to be avoided, nations needed to create economic interdependence and trade essential supplies with one another. The thinking was if one country had to lean on another for coal or steel or wheat, it would be less likely to go to war with it. But these institutions would eventually come under pressure to serve the interests of American and European corporations as they spread into other parts of the world. They were pushed to adopt principles and policies that favoured the free market, an economic system based on supply and demand with little or no government control, and where prices are determined by unrestricted competition among privately owned businesses. Nation-states — often referred to as economies — would produce what they do best and this would churn out affordable food, clothes and goods through a seamless web of global supply chains for a global consumer market. In this brave new world, all boats would rise, from the big yachts of the wealthy to the little fishing boats of peasant communities.

Conservative economists and thinkers were ascendant at this time and influenced the policies of the wave of "New Right" governments determined to undo the postwar social security consensus. These included Great Britain's Margaret Thatcher, Ronald Reagan in the US and Brian Mulroney in

Canada as well as Latin American dictators such as Chile's Augusto Pinochet, sometimes referred to as the first "free-market fascist." These politicians believed that governments had grown too big and too expensive, that people were coddled and needed to become more self-sufficient and that workers and their wages were too protected, hampering competition and stifling entrepreneurial ingenuity. All that was required was for governments to get out of the way of the market and let it work its magic.

Thatcher famously said there is no such thing as society, only individuals and families "looking after themselves first." Her belief resonates today with right-wing populists. In November 2020, speaking to students at the University of Texas, American conservative pundit Ann Coulter described her views in similar language: "We have to take care of our own first — that's Trumpism."

Increasingly the Bretton Woods institutions adopted the principles and policies of what came to be known as the Washington Consensus, a term coined by British economist John Williamson in 1989. The Washington Consensus set out policies to "help" countries facing economic hardships that became deeply divisive and eventually led to a huge backlash in the Global South. The IMF and the World Bank, as well as several regional investment and development banks, imposed deep structural reform requirements in recipient countries based on liberalization, deregulation and privatization in exchange for funding and programs. They adopted the core tenets of the Washington Consensus: enhanced property rights protections; an end to foreign investment restrictions; the eradication of government policies and regulations that restricted the entry of foreign corporations, including in the natural resources sector; the removal of trade barriers such as quotas and tariffs; the privatization of state enterprises, including railways and energy companies; and competitive exchange rates friendly to foreign investment. These principles paved the way for extractive corporations and industrial farm operations from wealthy countries to set up shop in poor countries and gain access to the land and water resources, often while paying little or no taxes to the government.

Additionally, the World Bank and IMF imposed deep spending cuts in education and health care as conditions for aid, and introduced the notion of public-private partnerships, allowing foreign companies to "deliver" these services on a for-profit basis. And they dropped any pretense of supporting full employment policies in the Global South. Given the system's emphasis on exports, poor countries turned to foreign investment with cheap labour and lax environmental rules.

Corporations win — for now

The 1980s also saw the birth of the think tank as an instrument of public policy. Prior to that time, conservative lobbyists were either dealing with issues of foreign affairs and the economy, or trying to influence government policy on behalf of a particular industry. But the Reagan/ Thatcher years saw the blossoming of conservative think tanks that had the postwar welfare state in their sights, and they came to wield enormous power with governments of all stripes. The American Enterprise Institute, the Cato Institute and the Heritage Institute in the US, the Institute of Economic Affairs and others in Great Britain and the Fraser Institute and the Business Council of Canada (then known as the Business Council on National Issues) influenced both conservative and neoliberal administrations in these and many other countries, halting the growth of a half century of progressive social policy.

All of this coincided with the rise of the transnational corporation, whose interests this system served. These are companies that might have administrative offices in one country, source their raw material in others, conduct their manufacturing and production in yet others and invest around the world. Their economic power is immense and pressures governments to create business-friendly policies. They also hide their profits in tax havens, robbing governments of much-needed tax revenues for social programs and infrastructure. In November 2020, the UK's Tax Justice Network reported that countries around the world are losing over C$560 billion in revenues every year to tax havens and private tax evasion.

Oxfam and the British social justice organization Global Justice Now have documented the rise of transnational corporations: of the top 100 economies in the world, 69 are corporations and only 31 are nation-states. Apple's revenues exceed the GDP of two-thirds of the world's countries. Exxon is bigger than India. Walmart's revenues exceed the GDP of 157 countries, including Spain and Australia. BP is bigger than Russia. China's National

Petroleum corporation is bigger than Mexico. The latter decades of the 20th century and the first two of the 21st saw a huge transfer of power from nation-states to transnational corporations.

The results of this experiment are appalling. The United Nations reports that in 2020 barely one in four working-age people around the planet has a stable job. Everyone else is part of the "precariat" — either unemployed or working in part-time and low-wage jobs with little security and few benefits.

One-quarter of the world's workforce earns around $2 a day. Some herald this statistic as a reduction in global poverty, as that is a slight improvement in recent years, but a scathing July 2020 report by Philip Alston, the outgoing UN special rapporteur on extreme poverty and human rights, says otherwise. The World Bank sets the international poverty line at $1.90 per day. Alston says the bank's definition reflects a "staggeringly" low standard of living, well below any reasonable conception of a life with dignity.

The precariat is not limited to the Global South. Startling figures in Europe and North America find the trend growing everywhere, as is inequality. In her 2018 book, *Oneness vs the 1%*, Vandana Shiva reports that in 2010, 388 billionaires controlled as much wealth as the bottom half of humanity. But the money became even more concentrated, and in 2018, that same level of wealth was held by just five billionaires. By 2020, 12 American billionaires had amassed a combined wealth of $1 trillion, many made richer by the COVID pandemic. In January 2021, the BBC reported that the wealth increase of just ten men around the world during the first year of the pandemic could have paid for vaccines for everyone on Earth.

Free trade changes my life

My entree into this world was the announcement in 1985 that Canada and the United States were going to negotiate what was really the first modern free trade agreement, the Canada–US Free Trade Agreement. It set me on a road I could never have foreseen. I was to learn that free trade was the most powerful tool in the economic globalization toolbox, one that would set enforceable global rules on every aspect of our lives. And the first experiment was to involve my country.

In December 1984, only months after being sworn in, Canadian Prime Minister Brian Mulroney laid out the argument for a free trade agreement with the US to the members of the Economic Club of New York. He announced that he intended to take Canada in a new direction — "open for business," he called it — and would lay out the welcome mat for American investors. The same day, his government took out a glossy nine-page ad in the *New York Times* outlining his plans to loosen foreign investment rules for American investors, gut the energy protections that gave Canada control over its energy resources and establish new ties in military coop-eration with the Reagan administration. The ad promised American companies could take 100% of their profits out of Canada, and boasted that Canadian wage settlements were being "dramatically decelerated." Canada's raw resources were used as a lure; the ad openly touted that the new government was happy with the high level of foreign ownership in its manufacturing and resources sectors. It brightly pointed out the advantages to American business of the fact that Canada sells raw resources to the US and then reimports American manufactured goods, thereby creating millions of American jobs.

Through his free trade agreement with the United States, which came into effect January 2, 1988, and his other free market policies, Mulroney changed the face of Canada. He dismantled Canadian control over the country's energy resources, gutted foreign investment screening, allowed American business to shutter their Canadian manufacturing subsidiaries without penalty, cut social security programs and unemployment insurance, gave giant American drug companies new patent rights, privatized much of the country's transportation system and attacked farm marketing boards.

Five years later, the deal was revised to include Mexico with the signing of the North American Free Trade Agreement, becoming the blueprint for a rash of free trade agreements around the world. With time, NAFTA would integrate the economies of the three countries, using wage competitiveness and deregulation to create common supply chains and produce cheap consumer goods.

The changes these free trade deals made to Canada have been well documented. Manufacturing in Canada was gutted as head offices shut down branch plants and jobs went to the low-wage US states and Mexico. Unifor, the private sector union representing auto workers, estimates that the auto sector alone lost at least 30,000 direct jobs, as well as countless others that served the industry. Combined with outsourcing to China and other low-wage countries, the gutted manufacturing in Canada left successive governments dependent on exporting raw resources. According to the Canadian government, as a percentage of Canadian GDP, manufacturing declined from 26% in the late 1960s to less than 10% today. This increased job insecurity and precarious work, wage stagnation, the hollowing out of the middle class, and wealth inequality.

For Canadians who were too young to have experienced these years, it is hard to describe how passionately debated these trade agreements were. The Canada–US Free Trade Agreement was the sole issue of the 1988 federal election. My concern and first reason for involvement was that American social programs were inferior to Canadian ones and I worried that harmonization of our economies and standards would threaten social security, particularly for women. I, like millions of Canadians, experienced a steep learning curve and came to believe that my values of peace and justice were deeply at odds with this agenda.

In 1986, a number of well-known writers, artists, labour leaders and academics formed the Council of Canadians, a social and environmental justice movement I would lead for over three decades. Our first task was to take a complex trade agreement and put it in language accessible to everyone, and flood people's mail and phones with the information. I set out across the country and spoke to hundreds of communities. I was stunned to see theatres and lecture halls filled to overflow. We were having a debate about the soul of our country and everyone knew it.

The Council of Canadians brought together organizations from many areas — labour, women, faith-based, Indigenous, agriculture, environment, anti-poverty, art and many more — into a network called the Action Canada Network. Action Canada's purpose was to coordinate research and disseminate information to a population hungry for it. I even took part on a two-night CBC town hall debate on free trade that millions of Canadians tuned into.

There is no question that we had a profound impact on the public discourse. When free trade was first introduced to Canadians, a majority were in favour. But the more they learned about it, the more concerned they became and, by the 1988 election, a majority of Canadians were opposed. There were two parties opposed to the deal and one party in favour. The election vote split between the Liberals and the NDP, who were the two against the deal, winning the election for Mulroney's Conservatives and allowing them to move ahead with their agenda. The Liberals were critical of NAFTA but nonetheless ratified it when they came to power in 1993.

I learned so much from this time. One thing was that you had to find a way to make a complicated issue simple, and you really had to know your subject. I read those trade agreements cover to cover and studied everything I could to learn about what both sides had to say on them. We wrote reports and submissions to standing committees, and over time, I would come to write many books on various aspects of free trade and corporate rule. But we also turned out op-eds, fact sheets and even comic books to reach as many people and sectors as possible.

I learned that directly lobbying elected MPs was not a great use of my time. They knew where we stood, and what mattered most to them was what their voting constituents thought. I discovered that it is more effective politically to reach as many people and communities as possible and persuade them of your position. They, in turn, reach out to their elected officials — the more the better. With this in mind, the Council of Canadians created dozens of grassroots chapters across the country that conducted research on local issues, held town hall meetings, lobbied local politicians, did media outreach and leafleted door to door. To fight NAFTA, we developed close ties with communities and groups in the US and Mexico as well.

This is when I learned how to use the media. Many of today's activists have given up on the mainstream media, as they feel it is too corporate controlled. They prefer to deal with alternative and social media. I am a big supporter of progressive news sources, but I also know that many people still get their news from local newspapers and radio, and we ignore that at our peril. At the height of the free trade fight, we were aware that both government and big business were wining and dining high-profile media commentators and saw their full-page ads in major newspapers. We could not allow that to go unchallenged.

We ramped up our press conferences and meetings with reporters and found that when we were creative, we could get a lot of attention. At the NAFTA signing (symbolic because it still had to be ratified by Parliament), a group of us disrupted the Canadian ceremony held in the beautiful, historic Railway Committee Room of the House of Commons and got "escorted" out by security guards. One member of our group actually walked up behind Prime Minister Mulroney as he was about to sign the deal and pulled the American flag over the Canadian and Mexican flags. The ceremony attracted a lot of media attention and the Stars and Stripes was the cheeky backdrop for all the photos taken that day, dominating coverage around the world.

And hope! I learned the value of projecting hope when you are losing. It hurt to mount the campaigns that changed hearts and minds but still lose the battle. We had put forward arguments that convinced the majority of Canadians that these trade agreements were not in their best interests, but we got sabotaged by politics and the sheer might of the corporate community and its influence with governments. I started to realize what we were truly up against and how long and difficult this struggle would be. I knew that an essential part of my role was to keep people hopeful and committed for the long haul.

I learned the value of projecting hope when you are losing.

The organizations and alliances we built to fight the trade agreements went on to address many other issues, including tax reform, public health, poverty, justice for First Nations, the human right to water, energy pipelines and the climate crisis. Jumping into these campaigns and building this movement kept me from the depression of losing a campaign we had really won. Another lesson: keep moving.

The fight goes global

While these political dramas were unfolding in Canada, the New Right and corporate lobbies around the world were busy promoting bilateral, regional and international free trade agreements. Big business wanted to be able to move their production to low-wage countries and pay no penalty. They also wanted what they called a "level playing field" so that they wouldn't have to bump into different standards and rules as they crossed borders. It came as no surprise that they fought to set low standards on such issues as health and safety, environmental protection and workers' rights.

Another lesson: keep moving.

They, and wealthy countries of the North, also wanted easy access to the raw resources of the Global South and the removal of export controls on fish, lumber, agriculture, minerals and energy. And they wanted access to the patent rights (called intellectual property rights) of seeds and plants on lands still largely held by small farmers, peasants and Indigenous peoples in poor countries. Free trade gave them all this and more.

To truly understand modern free trade agreements, says Haley Sweetland Edwards, a *TIME* correspondent and author of the 2016 book, *Shadow Courts: The Tribunals That Rule Global Trade*, we need to stop thinking that they are about trade. By the time the Uruguay Round of international trade negotiation was launched in 1982, she writes, free trade was almost exclusively about rules, the "nontariff barriers" that impede the movement of goods and services across borders. Which government standards, laws, regulations and practices were getting in the way of a global market in goods and services, and how should they be eliminated or at least harmonized? In the long run, she asserts, free trade deals were created to limit what governments can do and what rules they can establish. And the goal was (and still is) almost always deregulation.

The World Trade Organization (WTO) was established in 1995. Its website makes no pretense that its goals were about anything less than global market rules. "It took seven and half years, almost twice the original schedule," the site reports. "By the end, 123 countries were taking part. It covered almost all trade, from toothbrushes to pleasure boats, from banking to telecommunications, from the genes of wild rice to AIDS treatments. It was quite simply the largest trade negotiation ever, and most probably the largest negotiation of any kind in history."

In the years since the founding of the WTO, free trade has exploded. In 1990, there were 50 regional free trade agreements (deals between two or more countries) in force. As of the end of 2020, according to the WTO, there are now 420, 306 of which are what are considered "deep," as they cover a set of government policy areas beyond simple border controls.

Recent years have also seen the creation of large trading blocs, such as the United States–Mexico–Canada

Agreement, the Central American Free Trade Agreement, the Comprehensive and Progressive Agreement for Trans-Pacific Partnership, the Canada–European Union Comprehensive Economic and Trade Agreement, the African Continental Free Trade Agreement and the largest of them all, signed in late 2020, the Regional Comprehensive Economic Partnership. The latter covers about 30% of the world's populations as it includes 10 Southeast Asian nations plus China, Australia, South Korea, Japan and New Zealand.

Although they vary in the details, most free trade agreements make it hard for governments to favour domestic production and services or hire locally, and they require governments to open much of their markets to foreign competitors. This will always advantage the wealthier countries with the biggest corporations. Government laws and standards must be "no more trade restrictive than necessary" and can be challenged with binding dispute mechanisms and serious penalties if they are deemed "protectionist."

While public services can be exempted, once they begin to be privatized they become subject to the rules of the trade deals permanently. It is then very hard to go back if future governments decide that the privatization of, say, water services or health care was a mistake. To do so may require paying compensation to the private companies that have been replaced. And most recent trade agreements actually build in a process that formally includes the private sector to harmonize regulations and standards in many areas, including health and safety rules, working conditions and environmental protection.

Opposition goes global too

It was clear by the mid-1990s that the forces promoting free trade and economic globalization had gone global, having established international lobbies and interconnected think tanks that held great sway over governments and institutions such as the World Bank and even the United Nations. The notion of the inevitability of globalization was so widespread in academic, political, media and corporate circles, that questioning it showed you were parochial, nostalgic and out of touch.

David Korten is an American author, former professor at the Harvard Business School and vocal critic of economic globalization. In his extensive travels, he found an almost universal feeling of alienation among ordinary working people from the dominant paradigm being fed to them by the elite. In his 1995 bestselling book, *When Corporations Rule the World*, Korten wrote, "It is often the people who live ordinary lives far removed from the corridors of power who have the clearest perception of what is really happening. Yet they are often reluctant to speak openly of what they believe in their hearts to be true. It is too frightening and differs too dramatically from what those with more impressive credentials and access to the media are saying. Their suppressed insights may have them feeling isolated and helpless. The questions nag: Are things really as bad as they seem to me? Why didn't others seem to see it? Am I stupid? Am I being intentionally misinformed? Is there anything I can do? What can anyone do?"

It was clearly time for a coordinated international response to the free market juggernaut. The movements inside countries that had formed to resist free trade agreements, including the ones I worked with in Canada, realized that they were going to have to look beyond domestic borders and coordinate efforts if people were to stand a chance of challenging the hegemony of the narrative.

> It is often the people who live ordinary lives far removed from the corridors of power who have the clearest perception of what is really happening.
>
> — DAVID KORTEN

In 1993, I was invited to a meeting in San Francisco by Jerry Mander, a respected American writer and organizer. There, a group of activists, writers, thinkers and environmental and labour leaders founded the International Forum on Globalization, our first alternative think tank. We published documents and studies on all aspects of trade and globalization and disseminated them through our organizations back home. We revived the 1960s notion of the teach-in and held packed large-scale, three-day public events at many major gatherings.

Our first teach-in took place in November 1995, at the historic Riverside Church in New York City, where Martin Luther King Jr. once preached. Twenty-five hundred people lined up to attend, clearly seeking a place for learning, sharing, reflection and action. I will always remember the thrill of standing at the podium where King had stood, eager to help build a movement to change the course of history.

We would go on to have major teach-ins at many gatherings of the global elite, including the 1996 Asia-Pacific Economic Cooperation Forum (which set the stage for a regional free trade deal) in Manila, Philippines, all of the ministerial meetings of the World Trade Organization and the Earth Summit in Johannesburg, South Africa, in 2002.

We also formed Our World Is Not for Sale, a network of social movements and organizations that would coordinate the work of the many nation-based campaigns fighting local free trade agreements, as well as share research and analysis. The goal was to help shape an alternative international trade agenda that supported human rights, environmental sustainability and democratic principles.

To achieve this goal, it was imperative we create more progressive think tanks. Some were new, some were established but now turned their attention to the free trade agenda. In Canada, we came to depend on the Canadian Centre for Policy Alternatives. The Institute for Policy Studies and Public Citizen's Global Trade Watch were indispensable in the US, as were Global Justice Now in the UK, and Corporate Europe Observatory and Transnational Institute in Europe. Along with the Australian Free Trade and Investment Network, they all worked with Focus on the Global South and Third World Network in Asia and others in the Global South to provide background research as these new trade deals rolled out.

We were clear in our commitment to non-violence. Putting yourself and your safety on the line is one thing;

endangering others is never acceptable. While this commitment was not always honoured by all (and is not to this day in some street demonstrations), our movement had adopted the six principles of non-violence laid down by Martin Luther King Jr. Non-violence, he wrote, is a way of life for courageous people. It seeks to win friendship and understanding. It aims to defeat injustice, not people. Non-violence holds that suffering can educate and transform. And it always chooses love over hate (or indifference). Finally non-violence believes that the universe is on the side of justice and will eventually prevail.

I believe that non-violence as a tenet of activism is a testament to hope.

I believe that non-violence as a tenet of activism is a testament to hope.

First (sweet) victory

In October 1997, I travelled to Paris as part of a large delegation at the invitation of the Organisation for Economic Co-operation and Development (OECD). We went to show our opposition to the largest global investment liberalization treaty ever negotiated. It was called the Multilateral Agreement on Investment (MAI) and would establish a new body of universal investment laws to grant corporations unconditional rights to engage in financial operations around the world and to sue governments if national health, labour or environmental legislation threatened their interests.

The MAI had been negotiated behind closed doors and, by the time of this meeting, the governments were nearing the end of their negotiations. Taken aback by the ferocity of opposition we had mounted to the proposed deal, governments invited their civil society advocates to Paris to "explain" the deal, a pretense of consultation that was, for them, just a formality.

The OECD is the club of powerful nation-state "economies," now with 37 members, committed to the goal of stimulating a global economy through world trade. Founded in 1961, its member states account for 88% of world trade and investment. It is housed in a huge estate in the elegant 16th arrondissement of Paris, once the stately palace of Baron Rothschild. In a sumptuous, high-ceilinged boardroom and sitting on red velvet chairs with vast crystal chandeliers lighting our deliberations, an international delegation of civil society groups sat down with our governments' negotiators to tell them with one voice that we would fight their deal to the end.

For decades, the protection of foreign investors was a subject of debate at the UN. Large mining, energy and other companies from wealthy countries were seeking assurance that their investments would not be expropriated by a change of government if they set up shop in poor countries. As far back as 1959, to protect the investments of their corporations, a few wealthy countries signed investment agreements with poorer ones dictating the terms of compensation if the contracts were broken.

But most countries of the Global South resisted giving special protection to foreign transnationals, and in 1974 won the "inalienable right" to regulate and exercise authority over foreign investors with the signing of the UN Charter of Economic Rights and Duties of States. Transnationals could not intervene in the internal affairs of the host state, which retained the right to cancel contracts without penalty. The big mining, energy and agriculture corporations, however, had never given up their desire that investor-state rights be formalized in trade and investment agreements. And, in the intervening years, they were joined by the growing services sector lobby, also seeking global expansion.

They were pleased when Canada, the US and Mexico included an Investor-State Dispute Settlement (ISDS) provision in NAFTA, essentially giving North American corporations rights usually reserved for nation-states. In the Canada–US Free Trade Agreement, if a company or industry sector in, say, the US had a concern about its treatment in Canada or Mexico, it had to get the American government to lodge a complaint or go to the domestic court of the other countries. Now, for the first time, a major trade agreement — involving a superpower — was granting all the corporations of the signatory countries the right to directly challenge the policies, regulations, laws and practices of their governments.

The ISDS in NAFTA allowed the big corporations of the continent — mainly American — to seek compensation if they felt they had been treated unfairly. It established a legal process that foreign corporations could use outside the courts, one closed to domestic companies, giving foreign corporations new ability to affect the policies of sovereign governments. Arbitration was to go to a three-person tribunal made up of trade lawyers and experts.

Now free market governments and their business lobbies decided to press for a larger agreement with more players, and where better to take their campaign than to the OECD — the club of wealthy countries. Next would be the World Trade Organization, where they were confident corporations would be granted safe access to the considerable resources of poor countries. It was argued that giving transnational corporations these new rights was the price the governments of the Global South had to pay in exchange for desperately needed investment.

I had found out about the proposed MAI at a meeting of the International Forum on Globalization in early 1996. Armed with bits and pieces of information that our movement could glean from different sources inside the OECD, I wrote an op-ed demanding to know whether the Canadian government was part of this development.

The government denied any knowledge of such negotiations until, one day, we received the full text of the deal in a brown paper bag and were able to show that the Chrétien government was negotiating this deal behind closed doors with Canada's biggest business lobbies. The issue hit the front pages and stayed there for the next year while we mobilized opposition in Canada and around the world. Not since the heady days of the first free trade deal more than a decade earlier had Canadians shown such concern about an economic treaty.

We called it the Corporate Rule Treaty and held packed town hall meetings right across the country. We wrote analyses of the impact the MAI would have on Indigenous people, workers, culture, the environment, natural resources and women. We held regular press conferences, got many municipal councils to adopt anti-MAI resolutions and created more than 600 "MAI-Free Zones" in places as diverse as libraries, stores, seniors' residences and university campuses. We forced the government to hold hearings on the MAI and the testy exchanges revealed a defensive government.

Similar opposition was growing in other countries. Huge demonstrations were held in Paris and Berlin, and in March 1998, the European Parliament adopted a resolution urging its members to reject the MAI in its present form. Weeks later, one after another, key governments backed out of the deal: France first, then Germany, then Canada. The MAI was dead. Headlines around the world credited our movement for its defeat and praised our use of the internet. It was the first international campaign to use this new technology to such effect.

The *Globe and Mail* wrote that high-powered politicians were no match for this "global band of grassroots organizations," and that international negotiations of the future had been "transformed" by this development. The *Financial Times* compared the fear and bewilderment that seized the governments of the OECD to a scene from *Butch Cassidy and the Sundance Kid*, where politicians and diplomats looked behind them at "the horde of vigilantes in hot pursuit whose motives and methods are only dimly understood in most national capitals," and asked despairingly, "Who are these guys?" The *Globe*'s Report on Business said that while the negotiators were busy tending to Brussels, Geneva and Paris, our movement was tending to Kamloops, Saskatoon and Fredericton. "The lesson to trade gurus: stop thinking Paris and start thinking Kamloops."

It was a spectacular victory, and we were thrilled and empowered. But every victory creates a backlash and the push for corporate rights never waned, simply went underground for a while. Wealthy countries and their corporate lobbies continued the campaign inside the World Trade Organization and promoted bilateral investment treaties (BITs), investment deals between two countries. There are now over 3,000 bilateral investment treaties in the world, most between a powerful country using its clout to guarantee rights of access for its corporations to a less powerful country. Most contain ISDS clauses.

As of end of the 2021 fiscal year, there are well over 1,200 ISDS challenges, most of which were heard by the World Bank's International Centre for Settlement of Investment Disputes. Most cases have found in favour of the foreign corporation, and the great majority are laid against poor countries in Latin America, the Caribbean, Africa and Central Asia.

The compensation settlements sought and given have expanded dramatically in the last two decades. Now it is not unusual for a poor country to pay out compensation in the billions. Pakistan was ordered to pay an Australian mining company US$5.8 billion — 25 times what the company had invested in the project. An American underwater exploration company is suing Mexico for over US$2 billion because it disputes that country's environmental assessment of the project. Ecuador was ordered to pay Occidental Petroleum over US$2 billion when it seized an oil field the company had sold to China without the permission of the Ecuadorian government. The Washington-based Institute for Policy Studies reports that governments have been ordered to pay at least US$72.4 billion to foreign corporations in just the cases that are known (there is a lot of secrecy surrounding these lawsuits) and just for disputes over mining, gas and oil projects. There are cases pending in those sectors for another US$75 billion.

We didn't ask for a seat at the OECD table; we built our own table and forced governments to deal with us as a new political force.

All this was still to come, but back in 1998, we tasted victory and felt hopeful. Labour, justice and environmental groups separated by sector and geography coalesced into an international movement to fight economic globalization. We started to feel our power, knowing that our governments did not listen to us because we had good arguments, but because we had political clout.

We went into this and future debates with our own demands, our own analysis and our own vision. We didn't ask for a seat at the OECD table; we built our own table and forced governments to deal with us as a new political force. An important lesson.

Meera Karunananthan

Meera Karunananthan is an assistant professor at Carleton University and holds a PhD in geography. She served for a number of years as director of the Blue Planet Project, working with communities around the world on water rights.

Where do you find hope?

"I am deeply inspired by local struggles for water justice taking place around the world.

"When I first became involved in anti-globalization movements, I learned about the Cochabamba, Bolivia, water wars. Between December 1999 and April 2000, the people of Cochabamba took to the streets to protest the privatization of water services, which had led to exorbitant rate hikes. Community activists demonstrated for months, eventually forcing the Bolivian government to break its contract with the multinational Bechtel Corporation.

"Now twenty years later, I co-direct the Blue Planet Project with Marcela Olivera, who was a leader of the Cochabamba struggle. Together with our colleague Koni Benson in South Africa, we promote "trans-local solidarity" by supporting grassroots movements that are reclaiming their neighbourhoods, their public services and their power to protect local water sources from corporate theft.

"We work through global networks that bring together communities and grassroots movements not only fighting privatization, but also championing local alternatives. We provide not 'leadership' but connective tissue through platforms for information-sharing and collective knowledge building. We also bring an intersectional perspective to this fight, recognizing that the impacts of water privatization and corporate theft are deeply racialized, gendered and class-based. Through this work we support the multiplication of local strategies to reclaim communities from capitalism, patriarchy and racism."

Chasing the WTO

Seattle

In early December 1999, members of the World Trade Organization gathered in Seattle, Washington, to launch a new round of international trade negotiations. We were ready. For months our movements had been planning a coordinated opposition. "Turtles and Teamsters" — the first coalition between environmentalists and labour unions representing polluting industries such as trucking — came together in the "Battle of Seattle." We at the International Forum on Globalization held a teach-in at Benaroya Hall in the days preceding the meeting and filled the 2,500-seat concert venue, turning away hundreds more. The energy in that room was electric. I knew we were about to make history.

Upwards of 50,000 protesters descended on Seattle, surrounding the convention centre where the meetings were to be held, preventing the opening ceremonies and staging massive — and peaceful — demonstrations throughout the week. What ensued felt like a war zone. The Seattle police were unprepared and overwhelmed. They responded with tear gas, nerve gas, clubs, rubber bullets and concussion grenades. The mayor declared a state of emergency and imposed a curfew of 7 p.m. till 7 a.m., and the governor called in two battalions of the National Guard. Over 600 were arrested and many beaten in the violence that followed.

Inside the WTO, a battle of another kind was taking place. This was the first meeting of the WTO where poorer countries were included. Global South delegates demanded an inclusionary process and discussion on the power imbalance between the drivers of the WTO — the US, Canada, Japan and Europe — and the rest of the world. Tensions built and confrontations escalated. On December 3, President Clinton called the chair of the meeting and ordered it closed down. Three thousand media outlets from all over the world were there, reporting not on the glorious advancement of trade liberalization but on the protests, endangered sea turtles, sweatshops, child poverty, the plight of small farmers and the demands for the democratization of the WTO.

Several months later, the Rand Corporation published a report commissioned by the Pentagon that described our movement as a swarm of mosquitoes, with no headquarters, no clear structure and no leader, but who are everywhere and bite.

"Mosquitoes" continued to disrupt major gatherings promoting the free market agenda. Over 80,000 protesters descended on Quebec City in April 2001 for the summit of the 34 heads of state of the Americas who had gathered to promote a continental NAFTA-style agreement. To secure negotiators and officials, the government encircled most of the inner city with a three-metre-high concrete and wire barricade we called the "Wall of Shame." Summit officials were "protected" behind that barrier by 7,000 police (and thousands of soldiers on standby), who used armoured tanks, water cannons, plastic bullets and over 5,000 canisters of tear gas on protesters — the biggest security operation in peacetime Canadian history to that date. In spite of that massive show of force, the Free Trade Area of the Americas would fail four years later due to the organized opposition of Latin American civil society who were inspired by the showdown in Quebec City.

All through the summer of 2001, huge anti–free trade and anti-WTO protests were held in Europe, some of which were met with live bullets. One young demonstrator in Genoa, Italy, was killed. In spite of the fierce resistance we encountered, our pro-democracy movement was growing and we were filled with hope.

The Rand Corporation published a report that described our movement as a swarm of mosquitoes, with no headquarters, no clear structure and no leader, but who are everywhere and bite.

Our movement launched the World Social Forum (WSF) that year, an annual gathering of progressive civil society organizations and social movements from around the world. The purpose was to build solidarity and offer an alternative future to corporate-led economic globalization. The World Social Forum was held in January of each year at the same time as its rival, the World Economic Forum (WEC). The WEC brings the elite of the world to Davos, Switzerland, to promote public-private partnerships and free markets as the answer to the world's problems. The WSF has its origins in Latin American activism called the encuentro, meetings that emphasize dialogue and exchange of ideas among activists. Its motto became "Another world is possible."

The first WSF gatherings were held in Porto Alegre, Brazil, attended by 12,000 people. The forum continued to grow in 2004 with over 75,000 participants in Mumbai, India; 2005 with 155,000 back in Brazil; 2007 in Nairobi, Kenya, with 66,000 in attendance and 2011 in Dakar, Senegal, with 75,000.

Our success became its own problem, as the sheer numbers became unmanageable. Organizers realized smaller regional gatherings would work better and moved to that model. What we learned and shared at these meetings cannot be overestimated, nor the friends we made. It would stand us in good stead in the many international campaigns to come.

Doha

The next WTO ministerial meeting was held in Doha, Qatar, in November 2001. After Seattle, few other countries or cities wanted to host the WTO. From the point of view of those seeking to minimize the protests they now dreaded, the oil-rich emirate of Qatar was the perfect choice because of its low tolerance for political dissent. The WTO limited participation to one representative apiece for 600 international NGOs, 400 of which were business lobbies in favour of trade liberalization. The prohibitive cost of travel further cut our numbers and, in the end, only 100 civil society representatives made their way to Doha. We were assigned rooms in run down hotels far from the convention centre where the talks were held.

This was just two months after the 9/11 terrorist attacks on the US, and security for government officials and delegates was tight. Only a handful of Canadian civil society delegates were approved to attend, and no commercial flights were permitted into Qatar, so I had to fly on a Canadian Air Force Hercules transport plane with all the government negotiators and their big-business allies. Intimidating. The meeting itself was held in a luxurious compound built around the pyramid-shaped, gold-trimmed five-star Sheraton Doha overlooking palm trees, swimming pools and the azure-blue Persian Gulf. Tables laden with food were replenished around the clock.

Our group made the best of our limited numbers and the strict security, holding actions, dramas and creative demonstrations. In one, we taped our mouths shut and stood right outside the rooms where negotiations were taking place. (A Qatari security official told me that if it were not for the WTO having its meeting there, we would have been put in prison and the keys thrown away for such behaviour.) Our actions were intended to attract the media photographers and journalists who were shut out of official negotiations and eager for stories to send home. We also broadcast to the hundreds of thousands who held marches back home, and they spread our anti-WTO message far and wide. Doha would launch an ambitious new trade round called the Doha Development Agenda that promised to prioritize the concerns of the Global South.

Cancún

The next WTO ministerial was held in Cancún, Mexico, in September 2003. By then, the Global South had realized that the Doha promise of a "development round" was a lie. Their countries were being flooded with heavily subsidized agricultural products from Europe, Australia and North America. The subsidies allowed these goods to be sold on international markets at prices below the real cost of production, destroying the livelihoods of millions of small farmers in the Global South. Rich countries demanded market access to these poor countries before they would even start to cut subsidies to their own agricultural producers (many of which are large corporate conglomerates), creating an impasse.

So it was not surprising that the leaders of the protests in Cancún were farmers, many from Mexico and other Latin American countries, part of an international peasants' and farmers' movement called Via Campesina. Fearful of protests, the Mexican government had closed off the main highway leading into Cancún, a resort area served by thousands of workers who could not afford to live there and who commuted to their workplaces on this highway. A tall barricade covered in barbed wire was built that became a symbol of the struggle and the scene of some intense confrontations between armed police and angry protesters.

The farmers' union of South Korea, who led many of the demonstrations that week, was a disciplined and passionate contingent led by Lee Kyung-hae, who had lost his own dairy farm to a flood of foreign imports. He had become an outspoken critic of the WTO and was at the forefront of his group at the protests, wearing a sign that said "WTO Kills Farmers." On September 10, in front of us all, Lee Kyung-hae climbed the barricade, shouted that the struggle must continue and stabbed himself in the heart. He died in hospital several hours later. Tensions dissolved between protestors and the police, and his devoted colleagues set up a shrine at the site that became sacred to us all. His death is a scene that will haunt me to the end of my days.

On the last day, upon a command from the Mexican farmers' union, thousands of protesters sat down and a hush came over the crowd. Then a Mexican farmer played John Lennon's "Imagine" on his ukulele, and led by Indigenous women, the South Korean farmers dismantled the barricade with the help and permission of local authorities and the police. It was a moment of intense pain and great hope. None of us would ever be the same.

The Cancún ministerial ended in utter failure for governments and corporations. Not only did the wealthy countries refuse to deal with the urgent issues of agriculture and poverty, they tried to put an ambitious new agenda on the table, including raising again the hated issue of ISDS protection for foreign companies. As one, the delegates of the Global South said no and walked out. Those of us in the convention centre when that happened sang "Money can't buy the world" to the tune of the Beatles' "Can't Buy Me Love." A photograph of me and several others in full voice made headlines around the world.

Hong Kong

Divisions were deep and the tensions high as delegates from 149 countries met in Hong Kong in December 2005 for the next meeting. To observe a WTO gathering is to see the inequalities of the world on full display. The delegations of the powerful countries are in the hundreds, with ministers and other elected officials, principal negotiators and back-up negotiators, government advisors, lawyers, experts on call and spin doctors for messaging and the media and, of course, corporate advisors and lobbyists, all supported by state-of-the-art technology and technicians. The poor countries have as few as two or three delegates, no experts, no spin doctors, and, at that time, not even cellphones.

Money can't buy the world.

Exhausted negotiators from the Global South were under pressure from the US and Europe to open their markets, and we heard from several delegates that they were threatened with an end to aid packages to their countries if they did not comply. In the end, most signed a ministerial declaration that organizers were quick to call a success. In reality, many poorer countries had been bullied into compliance in exchange for promises that would not be kept — and they would not forget.

But much of the real story of Hong Kong happened on the streets. Officials closed off one square kilometre around the brand new, heavily fortified Hong Kong Convention Centre and erected fences around it and the five-star hotels where delegates were staying. Closed-circuit TV monitored the large area, and schools and shops were closed.

Over 9,000 police ruthlessly enforced security for the meetings. Thousands of protesters held non-stop actions for the entire week, sometimes boarding the subway and handing out roses and information to the citizens of Hong Kong who had little public knowledge of the WTO. At other times they walked and knelt every few steps until their knees and hands were bleeding. One day, 25,000 local domestic workers — most from the Philippines and Indonesia — joined a huge march wearing masks so that their employers would not be able to identify them.

Most notable in their strength and courage were again the farmers' and peasants' movements from South Korea who, hundreds strong and with military precision, crossed an eight-lane highway that officials had failed to seal off and got right up to the doors of the convention centre. I was with them and remember watching a group of South Korean women in their exquisite white traditional hanbok dresses, dancing in formation when the tear gas was let loose a short distance away. Many people were hurt, and hundreds arrested. When I look at the recent crackdown on those protesting the takeover of Hong Kong by mainland China, I am reminded of stumbling blindly away from that attack, asking myself what kind of a world they were creating at that meeting that necessitated such brutality.

The struggle intensifies

In Canada, we were facing a whole new series of threats. Integration of the economies of North America was well under way, thanks to NAFTA, when the three governments decided to promote what they called "deep integration" — harmonized standards on goods and services, closer security ties and continental resource sharing. In March 2005, Canadian prime minister Paul Martin, Mexican president Vicente Fox and US president George W. Bush launched the Security and Prosperity Partnership of North America at a meeting in Waco, Texas. Accompanying the leaders were 30 CEOs of the largest corporations from each country who formed the North American Competitiveness Council. This council had been set up to advise the working groups on harmonizing policy in areas as diverse as energy, the environment, financial services, health and immigration. The leaders agreed to meet every year.

Our biggest concern was that the governments were reporting to the business lobbies of the continent and not to their respective elected legislatures in what was clearly a new trade agreement. When the three heads of state — still George W. Bush from the US, but now Felipe Calderón from Mexico and Stephen Harper from Canada — met in Montebello, Quebec, in August 2007, civil society organizations across the political spectrum criticized them for the secrecy of their agenda.

During a demonstration outside the meeting, a number of us discovered and exposed several undercover Quebec police officers posing as protesters, trying to provoke violence with rocks and taunts at their fellow police. When they were challenged as provocateurs, the "protesters" were handcuffed and "detained" by other police, but video of the soles of their boots as they were dragged away showed clearly that they were wearing standard police wear. This stunt made headlines across the continent and further damaged an already discredited process. In August 2009, the official website of the project was updated simply to say: "The Security and Prosperity Partnership of North America is no longer an active initiative. There will not be any updates on the site."

This was a sweet victory for me personally. I traversed the country, speaking out against the deal, and my book, *Too Close for Comfort: Canada's Future within Fortress North America*, was a national bestseller. While we were up against great odds, our movements had now stopped the Multilateral Agreement on Investment, the Free Trade Area of the Americas and the Security and Prosperity Partnership of North America. And the WTO was stalled. It was imperative that we keep up the fight as the forces in favour of free trade were still very strong and there were more deals — and more struggles — to come.

In 2008, two other major trade agreements were undertaken that would have far-reaching effects. The first was the Trans-Pacific Partnership and involved 12 countries: the US, Australia, Brunei, Chile, Japan, Malaysia, Mexico, New Zealand, Peru, Singapore, Vietnam and Canada. It was signed in 2016, but the US pulled out under President Trump the next year and the agreement could not be ratified. The remaining countries then negotiated a new trade agreement they called the Comprehensive and Progressive Agreement for Trans-Pacific Partnership (CPTPP), which entered into force in 2018. The other was the Canada–European Union Comprehensive Economic and Trade Agreement (CETA) that went into provisional effect in 2017, with the full ratification subject to the acceptance by all member nations of the controversial provisions on investor rights (ISDS).

Both agreements removed most remaining tariff barriers among the signatory nations. They contained controversial rules for non-tariff barriers as well, setting up regulatory harmonization among nations with very different standards. Negotiated in tandem with big business lobbies, both make bringing a service that was privatized back under public management almost impossible. And both include ISDS rights for corporations.

It was more difficult to get the Canadian public as interested in these two trade agreements as previous ones. There were several reasons for this. First, neither agreement involved the United States, which always sets off alarm bells in Canadian heads. Living next to a superpower has made Canadians sensitive to and defensive of our "differences," and ready to fight to hold on to our sovereign right to protect our resources, social programs, foreign policy and cultural institutions. But Brunei? Chile?

Second, the mainstream media had long ago accepted the dominant narrative that free trade is a good thing, despite the fact that Canada has been the trade loser in both agreements so far. It was hard to get critical media analysis of these deals even from the CBC. As well, the deals were negotiated behind very closed doors. The full text of CETA was not published until the day it was signed.

With CETA, many Canadians were more open to a deal with Europe due to its higher environmental and labour standards, trusting that a trade agreement would impact Canada positively. Although we were able to show how large corporations from North America and Europe would use the deal to lower standards across the board, we just could not drum up as much interest from the general public, although the labour movement was onside. That was not the case in the other countries of these deals, whose civil societies put up a fierce opposition. Large demonstrations were held in Australia and New Zealand against the original TPP and in European cities against CETA and a similar EU-US proposed deal. In October 2015, more than 250,000 demonstrators marched through the streets of Berlin opposing CETA.

While we may have failed to make a mark with the larger public here in Canada on these two trade deals, our work educated and mobilized whole new groups and communities in other countries who went on to affect future trade deals. Opposition to ISDS in Europe, for example, was so fierce that CETA has still not been fully ratified, as many countries have not agreed to the investment provision. On the other side of the world, many of the same groups that opposed the TPP went on to influence the recently signed Asia Pacific Regional Comprehensive Economic Partnership, successfully keeping investment rights for corporations out of the deal.

Opposition here in Canada and in other countries held both agreements up for years. In 2008, when I first publicly declared that there would be organized opposition to CETA in Canada, I was invited to meet the EU ambassador and other European ambassadors to Canada to explain what my concerns were. In the meeting, they told me that Prime Minister Harper had assured them there would be no objection to this deal and that it could be completed in two years. They also said that there was no opposition in Europe either, which at that time was true because no one had heard of it.

My Canadian colleagues and I spent a lot of time in Europe, working with amazing people fighting for democracy and against the large corporate lobbies of their bloc. Nothing is more satisfying than bonding over shared hard work and a beer at a pub or café at the end of a long day. In April 2015, I debated then German chancellor Angela Merkel in advance of a G7 summit. I found her to be thoughtful and was impressed by how open she was to my criticism.

Our tour of seven countries took my husband, Andrew, and me to Europe for over six weeks. Because we packed everything into one carry-on each, I only had one washable navy blue suit and several blouses with a variety of scarves. I would ask Andrew each day, "Now what do you think I should wear today?" He would suggest the navy blue suit.

Light at the end of the tunnel

Here is the crucial lesson on hope and building movements I learned from fighting economic globalization. As I wrote in the first chapter, we have to take the long view when we set out to make change of this magnitude. As the saying goes, plant the tree even if you will not live long enough to sit in its shade. Don't get discouraged.

If we are right, time will tell. While we need to set goals, such as defeating CETA, we must not despair if we lose one fight. If we build a movement — which we did — it will go on to have ramifications we cannot imagine. It is essential to understand that *progress is a process* that takes time and a shape we cannot foresee.

Looking now at these issues and institutions, it is clear that organized opposition to economic globalization has, in fact, had a huge impact. Mark Weisbrot is an economist with the respected Washington-based think tank Center for Economic and Policy Research. In his 2015 book, *Failed: What the "Experts" Got Wrong about the Global Economy*, he writes that, since 2000, the International Monetary Fund lost most of its influence in poorer countries. Before then, the IMF was Washington's most important avenue of influence over economic policy in the Global South, as it was the funding gatekeeper. Borrowing countries that did not meet the IMF conditions would not get money from the World Bank or the regional development banks or even the private sector. As well, through the IMF, the US Treasury Department was given a direct veto over major policy decisions in recipient countries.

But the medicine these countries had to take proved to be the undoing of the IMF. Policies failed that forced poor countries to abandon industrial planning and regulation of their economies in favour of free trade and allowing foreign capital unfettered access to their workers, markets and resources, and resistance to the influence of the IMF grew exponentially. This in turn, says Weisbrot, has meant a serious reduction in US power in the world, "an epoch-making change" in international relationships.

Similarly the World Trade Organization is now widely seen as ineffective, and not just because former US president Donald Trump had no time for it. Writing in December 2020 for the *New York Times*, where she serves on the editorial board, award-winning journalist Farah Stockman says the WTO is all washed up. "If the World Trade Organization were a person," she writes, "it would be that dude in the bar drinking the afternoon away in his business suit and wondering where it all went wrong. He used to be a big shot."

It is essential to understand that progress is a process that takes time and a shape we cannot foresee.

When the WTO was created, she says, faith in free markets was at a record high and the US and its allies embraced an "almost messianic" belief in the ability of unfettered capitalism to improve lives around the world. "Domestic laws and programs that got in the way of 'free trade' were swatted aside like cobwebs. The WTO has ordered countries to gut programs that encouraged renewable energy and laws that protected workers from unfair foreign competition, as if international commerce were more important than climate change and workers' rights." The institution helped create the crisis of global inequality, says Stockman, and, in its current form, is incapable of dealing with the enormous issues of our time, especially a world economy in tatters from a pandemic.

It's possible that the institution might be responding to the prolonged public criticism. In early 2021, the WTO appointed Ngozi Okonjo-Iweala as its new director-general. Okonjo-Iweala is a former Nigerian finance minister and the first woman and the first African to take this role. She is a passionate advocate for universal access to vaccines and the need to provide vaccine equality to poor countries. She is also vocal on the need for the WTO to address the connection between trade and the climate crisis, and she plans to strengthen cooperation between the WTO and other institutions, including civil society, to set a framework for dealing with problems of the "global commons."

But for me, the most exciting development has been the growing consensus against Investor State Dispute Settlement (ISDS) among civil society and governments around the world. There has been a backlash in much of Latin America. A decade ago, Bolivia, Ecuador and Venezuela opted out of the World Bank's dispute settlement court altogether, in spite of pressure from global financial interests. Brazil has never been party to an ISDS agreement, and Uruguay and Argentina are now reassessing their former investment treaties. Peruvian president Pedro Castillo ran in the June 2021 election on a promise to reform trade and tear up all ISDS agreements, saying they were created to serve transnational corporations and cover them in "cloaks of impunity." He proposes to establish an alternative South American system to deal with trade disputes that does not include the rights of private investors to challenge governments.

Although there is an ISDS provision in the Comprehensive and Progressive Agreement for Trans-Pacific

Partnership (formerly the TPP), five signatory countries, including New Zealand and Australia, have signed an agreement not to use ISDS against one another. Following a passionate civil society campaign, ISDS was dropped from the Regional Comprehensive Economic Partnership (RCEP), a huge victory. Australia has undertaken a review of all of its bilateral agreements, and India has launched a similar process, having already reformed its policies in 2016 that led to the cancellation of bilateral investment agreements with 57 countries. In March 2021, Pakistan announced it will scrap all of its bilateral investment treaties over concern that they are shrinking the government's policy space with respect to adopting measures in the public interest.

Opposition to ISDS in Europe is so widespread, the European Commission declared it "dead" in a 2017 fact sheet, and in 2019, EU member states terminated all ISDS arrangements among themselves. New free trade agreements with countries such as Australia and Japan have no mention of ISDS, and there is no provision for investor rights in the new post-Brexit deal between the UK and the EU. Tellingly, opposition to ISDS is still holding up full ratification of CETA in Europe with many countries, including Germany, Italy, France, Greece, Ireland and Netherlands, refusing to adopt these provisions of the agreement, so controversial are they with their citizens.

US Democrats are strongly opposed to ISDS and President Biden has publicly stated his opposition to "special tribunals for corporations." The United States–Mexico–Canada Agreement that replaced NAFTA in 2020 eliminates ISDS between Canada and the US altogether and strongly limits its reach between Mexico and the US. This was a major victory for the North American movements that organized to rid the new deal of this pernicious provision and a loss for the corporate lobbies of the continent.

Katherine Tai, Biden's trade representative, has promised to focus more on ensuring that trade deals protect American workers rather than exporters or consumers and said she wants to bring supply chains back home. In her February 2021 nomination hearing before the Senate Finance Committee, Tai said she would break with past trade policies that "pit one segment of our workers and our economy against another." In his first major foreign policy speech in March 2021, Secretary of State Antony J. Blinken said his views on free trade changed when he came to understand that free trade did not benefit all Americans and that it caused many "pain."

Meanwhile in January 2021, the United Nations Conference on Trade and Development reported that a majority (58%) of the new policies in 2020 around the world to do with investment tightened up, rather than opened up, foreign investment rules, a clear departure from the trend of earlier years. Because of COVID, many countries are reregulating access to their health and transportation sectors in particular.

Rethinking globalization

Clearly, the bloom is off the globalization rose, with even conservative media outlets such as *The Economist* and the *Financial Times* declaring it dead. Paul Krugman is an esteemed American economist, Nobel Prize winner and columnist with the *New York Times*. Throughout the 1990s, one would be hard pressed to find a greater cheerleader for free trade and economic globalization. But he has had a change of heart. In the aftermath of the financial crisis of 2008, Krugman declared that much of the past 30 years of macroeconomics as articulated by himself and his colleagues was "spectacularly useless at best, and positively harmful at worst." In an October 2019 *Bloomberg* op-ed titled "What Economists (Including Me) Got Wrong about Globalization," Krugman wrote that he and other mainstream economists missed a crucial part of the story in failing to foresee "hyper-globalization" that led to social and employment upheaval for millions of Americans.

In his 2020 book, *The Expendables: How the Middle Class Got Screwed by Globalization*, bestselling author and former chief economist at CIBC World Markets Jeff Rubin admits that the middle class got stuck with the bill for globalization. Real wages in North America have not risen since the 1970s, union membership has collapsed, full-time employment is beginning to look like a quaint idea from the distant past and the middle class is in retreat everywhere in the Global North. Rubin says the labour unions' prediction that NAFTA would lead to massive loss of manufacturing jobs in Canada and the US was correct, as was the fear that free trade and globalization would lead to inequality inside countries and among them. Prior to globalization, having a job was an exit from poverty.

But now, because many jobs are part time, minimum wage and dead end, a job can be a gateway to poverty.

In an August 2020 interview with the *Globe and Mail*, Rubin said that the failure of supply chains to deliver essential medical and other supplies during the COVID pandemic was a turning point for the narrative that the market can always deliver best. It became clear that governments had to intervene. "It shouldn't have taken a bat peeing on a pangolin to bring this into focus."

I am hopeful that this is a lesson Canada has learned. Our country once had a publicly owned, not-for-profit, internationally respected pharmaceutical company, Connaught Labs, that could have helped develop a vaccine for the coronavirus and ensure a Canadian supply if there was a global shortage. In a March 2020 column for the *Toronto Star*, journalist Linda McQuaig told the story of this remarkable facility, a "superstar in global medicine," and the part it played in creating and producing lifesaving treatments and vaccines that contributed to the end of diphtheria and smallpox. But Conservative prime minister Brian Mulroney, bitten by the free market bug, privatized Connaught Labs in the 1980s and it is now owned by a giant French pharmaceutical company.

COVID exposed the resulting gap in Canada's capacity to deal with pandemics and this led to a change of heart on the part of governments of all stripes. Ontario premier Doug Ford said his province would never be caught again without the domestic capacity to provide essential medicines for its people. Federal and provincial governments have come together to address this vulnerability.

The CBC reported in a January 2021 story that a long-term strategy to research and fund vaccines in Canada is being pursued and is a top priority for the federal government. With hundreds of millions of dollars in new funding, several teams are now building the infrastructure Canada needs for advanced vaccine research and production.

If any good can come from something so terrible, it is that COVID affirmed the need for activist government. It also underscored the importance of good public services, especially health care and water, as well as financial aid for those who lost their jobs, homes or livelihoods to the virus.

It is in no one's interest to revert to narrow nationalism and isolation.

The task now is to build something new. It is in no one's interest to revert to narrow nationalism and isolation. No one wants to end the international exchange of culture and music and food and ideas and science and travel. Clearly, almost every manufactured good we buy is made up of parts from all over the world and that is not about to change. The question is one of balance and the need to put human rights, respect for diversity and the protection of nature at the heart of all that we do. Maybe now that this narrative of the "free" market has been exposed, we are ready to move on.

CHAPTER FOUR

THE FIGHT FOR WATER JUSTICE

Anything else you are interested in is not going to happen if you cannot breathe the air and drink the water. Don't sit this one out! Do something! You are by accident of fate alive at an absolutely critical moment in the history of our planet.

CARL SAGAN

My water activism started, as did the other two phases of my life's work, in Canada and over a concern for the rights of Canadians. For years, activists had been fighting various schemes for the commercial export of Canadian water to the United States. The Great Recycling Northern Development Canal project, first introduced in the 1960s, would have built an aqueduct through the Great Lakes. A western route called the North American Water and Power Alliance proposed damming most rivers in British Columbia and diverting the water to the United States. There were at least seven other water-diversion projects floated in the 1960s and

'70s, including one supported by Quebec premier Robert Bourassa and later by Prime Minister Mulroney.

When I discovered that water "in all its forms, including mineral water, ice and snow" was included as a "tradable good" in the Canada–US Free Trade Agreement and then again in NAFTA, alarm bells went off. This is because everything that is listed as a good in a trade agreement is subject to its rules, which basically restrict governments from interfering in the "free" trade of that good.

To make matters worse, the latest trade agreements included new rules to ensure that Canadian resources commercially traded to the US could not be cut off or restricted unilaterally. At the time the concern was about oil and gas, as the US was a major importer of Canadian energy resources. Even before it signed the first agreement, the Mulroney government introduced legislation that essentially made Canada's energy a continental resource controlled by the market. Canada so far had managed to stop plans to export its water, but these trade agreements added a fresh urgency. If any provincial government were to commence the sale of bulk water to the US, the trade deals would make it very difficult for future governments to turn off the tap.

The startling facts about water

I was soon to enter a world I knew nothing about. I had never given any thought to water. It was simply something that came out of the tap when I needed it and it was clean and safe. (I now know that this was not true then and is still not true for many Indigenous communities in Canada that have suffered severe water issues for decades.) But as I learned more about the threat to Canada's water posed by economic globalization, privatization and deregulation, I started to look at water issues in the rest of the world. And the more I learned, the more alarmed I became.

I have since written extensively on the global water crisis in many books and reports and it is not my intention to reiterate all of the frightening statistics and warnings here. I will just give a snapshot of where we are in 2022.

The simple fact is that our planet has a limited amount of water and our demand for that water is growing exponentially. So much so that we are running out of accessible clean water. We have not taken care of water. We pollute our rivers, lake and streams. We extract groundwater at an unsustainable rate. We use multiple chemicals, hormones and pesticides to mass-produce food and manufactured goods and much of the waste ends up in our watersheds. Extractive industries such as mining and fossil fuels poison ground- and surface water. We divert water from where it is needed in the local ecosystem to cities and industrial farms, and we are damming the rivers of the world to death.

It is important to point out that our abuse of water is a major accelerant of the climate crisis. Water is, of course, affected by fossil fuel–driven climate change as it warms rivers and lakes, endangering aquatic life. But not enough attention is paid to the other way around. The removal of water from watersheds negatively affects the local hydrologic cycle, creating deserts and warming the local climate.

We could end every greenhouse gas emission tomorrow and we would still have a water crisis. Part of our climate crisis strategy must be the restoration of watersheds, along with protection of forests, wetlands and soil.

This water abuse is terrible for the planet and other species but is also the greatest human rights threat of our time. The United Nations calls water scarcity "the scourge of the Earth" and says that at the current rate of depletion and pollution, two-thirds of the world's people are likely to be living in water-stressed areas by 2025. Every day, more than two billion people around the world are forced to drink contaminated water. Diarrhea caused by contaminated water and poor sanitation kills a child under five every two minutes.

And the harm is not confined to the poor countries of the Global South. More than two million people in the United States lack running water and basic indoor plumbing, and about 15 million Americans have their water cut off each year due to their inability to pay rising water rates. The World Health Organization reports that 57 million people in Europe do not have piped water at home and 21 million still lack access to basic drinking water services.

As we all learned when COVID burst into our lives, one of the most important things we can do to fight the virus — and other pathogens — is to wash our hands with soap and warm water. But half the population of the world has no place to do this. Three-quarters of households, as well as nearly half of health-care facilities in poorer countries, lack access to clean water on site.

Water for sale

Because the planet is running out of accessible water, who makes the decisions about access is crucial. I learned early in the fight for water justice that a mighty contest has been taking place since the mid-1980s. On one side are those who believe that water is just a commodity, like oil and gas, and should be put on the open market for sale. For them, the free market is the best determinant of access and water is a commodity from which it is perfectly acceptable to profit. This view has been held at the highest levels of the World Bank and the IMF, as well as many governments and corporations, and is taught in elite business schools around the world. Late American oil tycoon T. Boone Pickens, who was also in the water business, told *Businessweek* in 2008, "There are people who want to buy the water when they need it. And the people who have the water to sell it. That's the blood, guts and feathers of the thing."

On the other side are those of us who believe that water is a human right and should not be denied because of an inability to pay for it. We also believe that water is a common heritage, like air and oceans, as well as a public trust. As such, all uses for a watershed must be responsible to a body that represents the community and sets a hierarchy of use whereby some uses of the water — such as for essential human needs and for ecosystem protection — will take preference over others. Public trust allows us to protect, preserve and even restore watersheds and aquifers so that they are not seen as commodities to be mined for private profit. There is a rich history of public trust in many countries.

The commodification of water takes many forms. One is the privatization of essential drinking water and wastewater services. Margaret Thatcher started the practice when she privatized the water services of England and Wales in 1987. Around that time the World Bank began to insist on water privatization as a condition of aid and would often choose the private water utility — often one of the two biggest, Suez and Veolia — and even negotiate the contract, almost always behind closed doors. Many municipalities, either desperate for funds or believing that the private sector could deliver essential services more efficiently, went this route. Yet studies show that private water services cost more, deliver less and cut corners. Water rates are steadily increasing in many parts of the world, resulting in water shut-offs for those who cannot make the payments.

Bottled water is another form of water commodification. Huge water corporations, such as Nestlé (which owns 47 brands of bottled water), Danone, Coca-Cola and PepsiCo, drain springs and aquifers, paying a pittance for it and making a fortune selling it. Despite the many public-awareness campaigns, people still buy one million plastic bottles of water every minute — so many that if you were to put the bottles bought annually end to end, they would reach halfway to the sun. We now know that microplastics are in all of our rivers, lakes and oceans as well as in the food we eat and our own bodies. We have no idea about the long-term implications of this plastic diet.

Some countries and local governments also commodify water by converting water licenses to water rights and allowing the "owners" to sell them on the open market. Australia did this in the early 1990s with the expectation that farmers would conserve their water use if they could profit by selling the excess. Instead, water speculators moved in to buy up water rights, driving the price of water so high that the government could not afford to buy it back during a severe drought.

Chile actually auctions off entire watersheds, often to foreign mining companies who buy the water for their tailings waste. Several western American states allow farmers and ranchers to sell their water rights to developers, turning water into a cash crop. Water pollution trading replaces regulations and fines with a system that allows companies to pay to pollute.

Water is commodified in other ways as well. Large-scale foreign agribusiness companies buy up huge swaths of land in Africa and other places and through multi-decade leases they gain control of its water for profit. The Gaia Foundation reports that across Latin America, Asia and Africa, watersheds are falling under the control of foreign mining companies who buy long-term access to local water sources. In Canada, the government amended the Fisheries Act to allow mining companies to have local lakes redesignated as "tailings impoundment areas" so they can dump their toxic waste without being subject to the environmental rules of the Act, essentially privatizing watersheds.

Many major banks and stock market companies have created fast-growing water portfolios. Global Water

Intelligence, the leading publisher of reports and research for the international private water market, predicts that by 2023, the value of the global water market will be almost US$1 trillion.

As frightening as this all is, there is more. In December 2020, a new chapter in water commodification opened when CME Group, the world's largest financial derivatives exchange company, launched the world's first futures market in water, opening up the planet's water to market speculation. This new futures market is linked to the water market in California, a major food-producing state living in the perpetual shadow of drought. The regular water market encourages investing in actual goods and services relating to water, such as desalination plants, private water service utilities, bottled water and the trading of water rights, but water futures trading takes it all one step further, allowing buyers and sellers to gamble on and barter a fixed price for the delivery of a fixed quantity of water at a future date.

Pedro Arrojo-Agudo, the United Nations special rapporteur on the human rights to safe drinking water and sanitation, decried this development in a statement released by the Office of the High Commissioner for Human Rights. He said a water futures market could lure speculators such as hedge funds and banks to bet on prices, repeating the speculative bubble of the food market in 2008. "In this context, the risk is that the large agricultural and industrial players and large-scale water utilities are the ones who can buy, marginalizing and impacting the vulnerable sectors of the economy such as small-scale farmers."

He added that water has a set of vital values for our society that market logic does not recognize and therefore cannot manage adequately, let alone in a financial space so prone to speculation.

Building a global water justice movement

It was while I was still fighting the impacts of economic globalization that I found myself helping to build an international water justice movement. In 2000, the Council of Canadians founded the Blue Planet Project, a global initiative based in Ottawa that works with partners around the world to achieve water justice based on the principles that water is a human right, a public trust and part of the global commons.

My travels around this initiative took me to every inhabited continent to meet with local groups and communities in solidarity with their struggles and to help build a movement where we could learn from and support one another. With time and effort, water justice groups and coalitions sprang up around the world and together we became a powerful network of activists, organizations and even government agencies. These include the People's Health Movement in South Africa, Food & Water Watch in the US, Friends of the Earth International, Red Vida of Latin America, Aqua Publica Europea, the European Water Movement and many national organizations in Europe, Focus on the Global South and Jubilee South and others in the Asia Pacific region, and Navdanya in India, among many others all over the world. We worked closely with one another and with the public sector unions inside each country as well as Public Services International, the global union federation representing 30 million public sector workers in 154 countries. Each organization worked inside their own regions and countries to protect local water sources, stop the privatization of water services, fight the contamination of watersheds by foreign mining companies, ban water extraction by the bottled water giants and prevent many other forms of water and human rights abuses.

We also went straight to the seat of power. The World Water Council is an international water policy think tank based in Marseille, France, that promotes water privatization and technological fixes to the water crisis. Its members include private water utilities, bottled water companies, water industry associations, water engineering firms and investment banks, as well as representatives of the World Bank. Its president, Loïc Fauchon, was an executive of a private water operators association in France that included the water giants Suez and Veolia.

Every three years, the council holds a lavish showcase for the water industry called the World Water Forum and our movement has followed and challenged them everywhere they have met, from the Hague, to Kyoto, Mexico City, Istanbul and Marseille. At first, a small number of us roamed the halls of their conventions, intervening where we could. With time, we could be more effective setting up our own alternative water forums that many thousands could attend. This aided the steady buildup of our movement. We also held seminars, workshops and debates at the annual World Social Forums, where we were able to bring many new groups and activists into the water struggle.

Turning the water commodification tide

We believed deeply that the United Nations had to recognize water and sanitation as fundamental human rights. Water had not been included in the 1948 Universal Declaration of Human Rights as it was not an issue at that time. But by the 1980s, it was becoming clear that the lack of access to clean water, particularly in the poor countries of the Global South, was a growing and horrific human rights crisis. The lack of a human rights designation for this crisis left untold millions on their own. Our water justice movement set a goal of adding water and sanitation to the list of fundamental human rights already recognized by the UN and we began lobbying seriously for this at the turn of the 21st century.

We chose this as a central goal because language matters. Naming the crisis as one of human rights would redefine it as an issue of justice, not charity. We believed that this would give communities fighting for their water rights a formidable new tool. Not surprisingly, the same interests that insisted water is a market commodity opposed our campaign. They defined access to water and sanitation as a "need" that could be met by government welfare, aid agencies and charities. In 2005, Peter Brabeck-Letmathe, then CEO of Nestlé, said that the notion of water as a human right was "extreme" and asserted that water is a foodstuff best valued and distributed by the free market. He has since walked back a bit on that position, stating that he would "set aside" 1.5% of the world's water for the poor and the rest would be put on the open market.

The opposition to our campaign was intense. Many governments worried that they would now be responsible to address the violations occurring in their countries. The government of Canada opposed the campaign because it rightly knew that if the UN were to formally recognize that water and sanitation are fundamental human rights, it would be held to account for the appalling condition of water services in First Nations communities. Some wealthy countries feared that they would be called upon to help fund these essential services in poorer countries if they voted in favour. The big private water utilities and bottled water companies, the World Bank and the World Water Council joined these countries in opposing this campaign.

Language matters. Naming the crisis as one of human rights would redefine it as an issue of justice, not charity.

But we prevailed. In 2008–09, I had the honour of serving as senior advisor on water to Miguel d'Escoto Brockmann, a Nicaraguan liberation theologian priest and the 63rd president of the United Nations General Assembly. We assembled a small group of allied countries and on July 28, 2010, Bolivian UN ambassador Pablo Solón Romero challenged the General Assembly to recognize the right to water and sanitation as "essential for the full enjoyment of the right to life." The vote was overwhelming: 122 countries voted in favour and 41 abstained. No country actually voted nay. Two months later, the UN Human

Rights Council defined what these new rights would mean and clearly spelled out the obligations they place on governments. It was a huge breakthrough.

Hard-fought victories

I said at the time that the nations of the world had decided that no one should have to watch their child die of water-borne disease just because they cannot pay for water. Humanity had just taken an evolutionary step forward. Of course, the UN resolution did not immediately alleviate the crisis for the billions suffering from lack of water. We are up against the perfect storm of declining clean water sources, rising water rates and growing inequality, within and among nations.

Nevertheless, very real progress has been achieved. Dozens of countries have either amended their constitutions or introduced new laws to affirm the human right to water and have implemented a plan of action to provide safe drinking water and sanitation to their people. The UN resolution has also been used in legal challenges against water shut-offs and other forms of water injustice. It was the basis for the European Citizens' Initiative — a direct democracy tool for citizens — getting the European Parliament to formally recognize water as a public good vital to human life. In one of many such examples, bending to public pressure, the Jakarta High Court of Indonesia evicted the private water companies in 2017 and ruled that the management of water systems "must be in accord with United Nations principles and values of human rights."

In a 2020 report on the tenth anniversary of the UN recognition of this new right, Léo Heller, former UN special rapporteur on the human rights to safe drinking water and sanitation, wrote that one clear achievement is that an increasing number of civil society organizations and grassroots movements have adopted the language of the human rights to water and sanitation in their formulations, analyses and, above all, their struggles on behalf of their most disadvantaged populations.

This, in turn, has encouraged civil society to monitor their governments' actions and to promote more public participation in decision-making processes. As a result, Heller reports, governments are well aware that they have the obligation, both moral and legal, to ensure safe drinking water and sanitation for all, without discrimination. "Having reached this awareness is a great milestone that took decades of efforts by many outstanding individuals and organizations."

Our movement was deeply engaged in fighting the privatization of water services and made the return of these failed experiments to public management a top priority as well. The Transnational Institute in Europe monitors these "remunicipalizations" around the world and reports that, since the year 2000, 334 municipalities that had tried privatizing their water services have taken them back under public control. It is particularly sweet that many of these have taken place in France, the home of Suez and Veolia, the two largest private water operators in the world.

Fights against bottled water operations have also been fierce. In 2010, worried about the Canadian government's promotion of water services privatization at that time, the Council of Canadians and the Canadian Union of Public Employees held a large gathering in Ottawa to sound the alarm on the looming commodification of Canada's water. I had long felt that we needed to have a positive campaign to promote the right to water and to protect local water sources. So at the event, we launched the Blue Communities Project, aimed at stopping the Canadian government from forcing water privatization on Canadian towns and cities.

A Blue Community takes three pledges: to protect and promote the human right to water, to assert that water is a public trust and therefore no privatization of water services will be allowed, and to phase out bottled water on municipal premises and at municipal events such as conferences and concerts. The campaign took off immediately and municipalities started signing up. While I never imagined this being anything but a Canadian initiative, it has since spread to Europe and beyond. There are now at least 60 Blue Community municipalities representing over 20 million people, and they range from small towns to some of the largest cities in the world, including Vancouver, Montreal, Brussels, Berlin, Paris and Los Angeles. Most of the European Blue Communities added a fourth commitment to promote public, not private, water services in their foreign aid work.

The project has also been adopted by unions, universities and faith-based communities. The World Council of Churches, representing 590 million Christians worldwide, became a Blue Community in 2016 and promotes the human right to water in its churches in 120 countries. Hopewell Avenue Public School in Ottawa, which several of my grandchildren attended, is to become the first elementary school to become a Blue Community in 2022 and the students and staff hope they set a trend for others to follow. When a school becomes a Blue Community, it presents an opportunity to learn about the looming water crisis and what people can do. Giving young people something positive they can work toward works wonders and gives hope.

Lesley Kathnelson is the Hopewell teacher behind the school's project. She says that young children and youth are passionate about effecting change and this project is a tangible way for them to make a difference. The students care about water, and through the deeper water education, they are coming to appreciate not only how fortunate they are to have clean water but also what needs to be done to ensure that everyone has the same access.

A Blue Community takes three pledges: to protect and promote the human right to water, to assert that water is a public trust and therefore no privatization of water services will be allowed, and to phase out bottled water on municipal premises and at municipal events such as conferences and concerts.

"Being a Blue Community is much more than a designation for us," she wrote me in an email. "It is a journey of learning about the human right to water, the importance of conservation and the opportunity to explore the effects of our own water consumption on the environment, especially with regard to bottled water." She says that having this work during the COVID-19 pandemic was a wonderful source of hope for teachers and students alike when so much felt so grim, and she notes, "We hope that our school is just the beginning of a movement toward all schools adopting this important learning around water."

The project has been successful in Canada in holding off the privatization of municipal water services and the Trudeau government ended the requirement, installed under Stephen Harper's Conservatives, of withholding federal funds to municipalities that refused to adopt public-private partnerships when fixing and expanding water infrastructure.

Another positive sign is the commitment to end long-term boil-water advisories in First Nations communities undertaken by the Trudeau government in its first term in office. While its goal to end them all by 2022 is not likely to happen, and there are still boil-water advisories in effect in 32 Indigenous communities, 108 have been lifted since 2015. A source of shame for all Canadians is being addressed with this work, and Canada's 2020 adoption of the United Nations Declaration on the Rights of Indigenous Peoples will help ensure that these injustices do not stand.

COVID lessons

The great author and human rights activist Arundhati Roy wrote of the COVID-19 crisis, "Historically, pandemics have forced humans to break with the past and imagine their world anew. This one is no different. It is a portal, a gateway between one world and the next." Just as the horrors of the Second World War led to a cry to define and protect inalienable human rights, it is my fervent hope that we have learned some hard lessons from the recent pandemic that can help us heal the planet and deal with inequality. COVID-19 shone the spotlight on the urgent need to address the lack of access to sanitation for half the world's population.

Already, there are signs that in addressing COVID-19, more permanent sanitation services are being installed where they are most needed. In a September 2020 edition of *The Lancet*, epidemiologist Dr. A. Kofi Amegah wrote of the "tremendous" improvements in access to handwashing facilities in schools, bus terminals, community centres and markets in many African countries. Moreover, some African governments have taken urgent steps to make clean water accessible to all communities, he reported, by drilling boreholes and mobilizing water tankers to supply water.

> *Historically, pandemics have forced humans to break with the past and imagine their world anew. This one is no different.*
> — ARUNDHATI ROY

UNICEF and the Stockholm International Water Institute also report that during the pandemic many countries have taken proactive steps to ensure water supplies and sanitation services, including reconnecting households who have had their water shut off and getting urgently needed water to migrant communities. The World Bank reports that Latin American governments have stepped up their water services to the most vulnerable, building handwashing and toilet facilities in many poor communities.

Christa Hecht

Christa Hecht served as managing director of the Alliance of Public Water Utilities in Germany and is currently the volunteer coordinator of the Blue Community movement in Germany.

Where do you find hope?

"The fight against water privatization in my country was long and hard. But because water in Germany belongs to all, right2water — our campaign against corporate control of water services — gained wide support among civil society organizations. One of the most intense fights was the remunicipalization of water services in Berlin, a response to a referendum in which the citizens of the city overwhelmingly rejected privatization. After that, the tide turned and almost all political parties now advocate for public control of water services in Germany.

"The COVID pandemic reminded me that former pandemics, such as typhus and cholera that were terrifying 180 years ago, were defeated by the delivery of public water for all. Clean water and sewage services, run by the municipality, became a matter of course. Now in this new crisis, many have once again realized how important public goods are."

The UN also launched a US$2 billion global humanitarian fund for sanitation and water services in the Global South to combat COVID-19. Charities such as Oxfam, aid agencies such as USAID, and wealthy countries such as Germany and Canada have targeted large portions of their COVID relief to permanent sanitation services in poor countries.

In the US, an NGO campaign convinced many states and cities to end water shut-offs as they violate the government's obligation to the human right to water and sanitation. At the campaign's peak in June 2020, reports Mary Grant, Public Water for All campaigner for Food & Water Watch, this campaign successfully protected two-thirds of the country from water shut-offs. After the 2020 election, citing the lives saved by the shut-off suspension, 600 organizations called on President Biden to implement a permanent nationwide moratorium on shut-offs to people who cannot pay their water bills, a demand made more urgent by the massive job losses and economic hardship due to the pandemic.

In April 2021, the US Senate approved a landmark $35 billion infrastructure bill giving the Environmental Protection Agency funds to upgrade the country's drinking water and wastewater systems. Recognizing that COVID-19 has hit disadvantaged communities harder, the Biden administration targeted them for priority water investments.

In his 2020 book, *Public Water and COVID-19: Dark Clouds and Silver Linings*, Queen's University political science professor David McDonald and his co-authors argue that COVID-19 has shown that public water operators are more able to cope with crisis than private water operators due to their ability to make plans and decisions based on long-term consequences rather than short-term profits. "We fundamentally believe that public water services can be more democratic, more accountable and more transparent than private water services, largely because they are not driven by narrow profit objectives. They also have better potential for collaboration with other public service providers given their broad public good mandates, and they have longer-term time horizons with regard to investments in people, infrastructure and systems where they work."

Notably, say the authors, the COVID-19 pandemic has revealed the "ugly underbelly" of poor water services in the wealthy countries of the Global North, leading to a more robust coalition of voices for change. The crisis gave rise to a new commitment to the concept of water as a public trust for all, everywhere.

Lessons learned

In helping build the global water justice movement and organize against economic globalization, I have learned some things I would like to share. The lessons from both efforts are intertwined.

Take the time it needs to build a movement

This is just plain hard — although joyful — work. To build the global water justice movement, I and my fellow water warriors spent years travelling to meet with groups and organizations fighting for water justice. We travelled to communities that were the victims of water injustice. It is crucial to make the effort to meet face to face. By doing this, you get to know and trust one another, and you learn how to work together. When you take the time to do this, it is easier to mobilize action around an issue that comes along, as the relationships are already there. You know who to go to for a specific statistic or report. You know who might have access to an important government official or some media in their city or country. You know who to contact to get the word out in communities where you might not have access.

Here in Canada, we worked with many local groups fighting to stop water privatization, bottled water extraction, quarries, oil pipelines or fracking operations. It's important to stay in the community while the protest is going on, and it means working shoulder to shoulder with the local activists. I am most proud of helping out on several important Indigenous fights, including the Tsilhqot'in of the area around Williams Lake, BC, against an open pit mine, the fight for basic water services by the Shoal Lake 40 First Nation near Kenora, Ontario, and the anti-fracking campaign by the Blood First Nation of southern Alberta. Sometimes crucial steps to movement building aren't related to the cause at all: we make great progress by just being there, sitting for long hours, breaking bread, getting to know one another, sharing stories, building relationships, offering financial or legal support.

And believe me, alliances, Canadian and international, built up over years, stood us in good stead when we could no longer meet in person due to the pandemic and had to connect for our work online.

It is important to take the time to come to a common analysis of the issue and a common framework for what you are asking. You can't hurry this. I remember many long meetings in places as diverse as Montevideo, Uruguay; Osaka, Japan; Nairobi, Kenya; Delhi, India; Berlin, Germany; and Melbourne, Australia, not to mention the many slums, townships and favelas of the Global South, where we struggled to come up with common language to describe our beliefs and demands and to articulate an actionable vision. What does public trust mean in different cultures? How do we define the commons? Who speaks for the community? How do we deal with issues of governance in places where governments are the enemy?

Take the time to come to a common analysis of the issue and a common framework for what you are asking.

Most importantly, building a movement is, *in and of itself*, a goal. While our issues and campaigns shift, so does the need for strong and progressive civil society movements that can grow and shift and adapt to meet new challenges. I find enormous comfort and pleasure in staying in touch with people I have worked with all over the world, on campaigns that were successful and those that were not. I believe that building a movement should be seen as a success even if the goal of the campaign was not achieved. Bringing new groups and people in, finding new friends, educating young people, sharing research — all this builds the kind of civil society needed for a healthy democracy.

Craft a clear message

A good politician will tell you that you have to find a clear, easy-to-understand message and repeat it until it becomes part of the narrative. It was vital that we clearly critiqued what was wrong with the growing acceptance of a market solution to the water crisis and counter it with our own. Crafting a simple message is far from a simple process: it takes a long time to come to consensus.

I cannot remember how many times I have written or have said in a speech that there is a "mighty contest" between those who see water as a commodity and those who see it as a commons. Those two simple words sum up the struggle over the future of water access, and make it clear that there are very different visions being proposed to deal with the growing human and ecological crisis. No mushy middle here.

In finding language that was clear and resonated with people's lived experiences, we were successful in getting our countermessage out. Even when they do not agree with us on the human right to water, professors in business schools in many countries now teach our perspective, if only to try to debunk it.

"Water for All," "Water Is a Human Right," "Water for Everyone, Everywhere," "Water Is a Public Trust," "No Water Shut-offs," "No to Water Privatization," "Take Back the Tap" are more than just slogans. These messages situate our movement within a larger critique of economic globalization and the market economy. They clarify where we stand on who gets to make decisions about access to water and in whose interests they do so. While few argue against the human right to water anymore — how could they? — there are powerful entities that use the concept to promote their interests and maintain the power imbalance. Bottled water companies agree that water is a human right and claim to deliver it as a service to humanity. Private water utilities pay lip service to the human right to water but argue that it is a "choice" of governments to use a public or private operator to deliver this "right." Those speculators setting up a water futures market do so in the name of water conservation.

In April 2010, I was at the University of Miami in a packed auditorium, sitting on a panel on the future of water. It was organized by the Clinton Global Initiative, and as I might have guessed with a foundation whose donors include Walmart, Dow Chemical, Goldman Sachs, ExxonMobil and Coca-Cola, the event promoted neoliberal market-based reforms dressed up in humanitarian language. A "compromise" was urged upon us so that more "ethical" private water companies would be welcome in the market. I used straightforward language and stated our position as clearly and simply as possible. After I spoke, students from Latin America rose to tell the story of water theft in their home countries and the suffering they and their families had endured. This — my simple speech and their powerful witness statements — is exactly what I mean when I say we are stronger together. Our voices united had a much deeper impact than either would have on their own.

Set clear goals and create an alternative vision

I have learned in my years of activism that people who care want to *do* something. They want to take action, and they will jump in to help build an alternative. Never tackle a "problem" without offering a solution, or at least a possible path to that solution. It can be as simple as encouraging people to sign a petition or write a letter to the editor of their local newspaper or an email to their elected official. Or the action could be much larger, such as getting city council to cancel a contract with a private water company or a provincial or state government to ban water-taking licenses for bottled water companies. It might

> *Never tackle a "problem" without offering a solution, or at least a possible path to that solution.*

mean working with many others to save a lake or river or wetland, a labour of love that may go beyond our lifetimes.

Often our activism needs to push for new or revised legislation. A vision of healthy watersheds inspires the demand for laws that ban dangerous chemicals and regulate the waste from farms and mines. We cannot leave this to chance or to corporations and the market to self-regulate. Martin Luther King Jr. said that legislation may not change the heart but it will restrain the heartless. Those in business with a conscience — and there are many — who want to respect human and worker rights and protect natural resources are at a disadvantage when they have to compete with companies that lower their costs by abusing people and the environment.

Our most successful campaigns have been built on a vision that excites people and makes them want to participate. The Blue Communities project has been a huge success because it speaks to the heart of what we want as a society and gives us a way to implement it. We have not always been able to depend on traditional media to report on our vision and our actions, so creating our own media outlets and social media presences has been crucial. So has being creative with our messages.

Our most successful campaigns have been built on a vision that excites people and makes them want to participate.

In July 2014, I joined the Windsor chapter of the Council of Canadians in a 12-vehicle convoy to Detroit, where we brought 750 gallons of Canadian public water to the residents there in a symbolic show of support for their fight against water shut-offs. After being stopped at the border by hostile American customs officers, we were met by grateful protesters who led our convoy through the downtown to a church that served as a water drop-off centre for the thousands of Detroit families without running water.

Of course the amount of water we brought did nothing to make a dent in the demand. But the symbolism of our gift was powerful, and we made news all over North America. Paul Moist, then president of the Canadian Union of Public Employees, was quoted in *USA Today*, saying, "America is better than this. If the richest county in the world can bail out banks and bail out Wall Street with public money, then public money from the state level and national level can be used to help the people of Detroit who are in harm's way health-wise without water." This was a great example of a concrete action that gave us a sense of purpose, showed cross-border solidarity and gained badly needed publicity for the people affected by the shut-offs.

Build bridges

The most effective movements include many sectors and create new alliances. This can only be done by listening to others and trying to bridge differences. It worries me that many young environmentalists have little connection to workers and their labour movements. Part of the problem is that some workers are employed by the very industries environmentalists are trying to shut down, such as fracking, mining and fossil-fuel auto manufacturing. As well, many environmentalists are not unionized themselves, working as they do for small NGOs. And the struggles of working people may not be top of mind when the environmentalists are working on climate chaos and species extinction. Several years ago, I spoke at a youth-oriented justice conference in Vancouver attended by over 1,000 young people. There were dozens of speakers and panelists, but not one was from the labour movement.

Conversely, some union leaders do not support "social movement unionism," the practice of engaging in wider political struggles for human rights, social justice, environmental sustainability and democracy. Some more traditional unions stick to organizing workers and fighting for workplace rights. This has led to a declining influence of unions on social issues, and increases the distance between them and younger activists. But I think that the most successful unions do see themselves as allies of social movements and they seek out justice, student, environmental and faith groups to work with on issues of mutual concern.

The most effective movements include many sectors and create new alliances. This can only be done by listening to others and trying to bridge differences.

I have worked closely with labour unions in Canada and internationally. I have taken many a town-hall tour with the leaders of the Canadian Labour Congress and its affiliates. I fought water and health privatization side by side with the Canadian Union of Public Employees. I fought bad trade agreements with Unifor and its predecessors, the Canadian Auto Workers and the Communications, Energy and Paperworkers Union. And I fought the big private water companies with Public Services International and its affiliates in many countries.

Labour unions often have the funds to mount a campaign and they can help struggling justice groups and smaller organizations get their message out to a wider public. And in a conservative or neoliberal political culture, unions are often a target of public anger and unfriendly elected officials. At these times, the support of the larger civil society is very important. Everyone is more vulnerable on their own.

Supporting the struggles of workers and their unions is crucial for the overall fight for justice. As we move to a precarious workforce with more workers having to take low-wage, insecure jobs — often more than one — we put many at risk who may not be able to afford housing and good food for their families. Many of the workers in these dead-end jobs are from minority groups, leading to further division and injustice in our society. The fight for robust unions is the fight for the empowerment of everyone and should be a key goal for activists. We need to support working people, and that means walking on their picket lines and standing in solidarity when their rights are threatened. That is not to say it is easy to agree. Where I have led, I have insisted that we hash out our concerns and come if not to agreement then to an understanding.

One example of this kind of cooperation is Blue Green Canada, an alliance of Canadian labour unions and environmental and civil society organizations that advocate for working people and the environment by promoting solutions to environmental issues that have positive employment and economic impacts. Another is the Green Economy Network, also an alliance between labour and civil society organizations, whose three pillars are clean, safe transportation; clean, renewable energy and greener buildings. The network recognizes that these initiatives would not only protect the environment but also create hundreds of thousands of jobs.

Ensure the movement is inclusive and confronts racism

I have watched the rise of the right in the United States with horror. While clearly historical and systemic racial discrimination is not new and has been faced by Indigenous Peoples, Jews, Blacks and people of colour for centuries, neo-Nazis, white supremacists, misogynistic and militaristic groups, such as Proud Boys and Oath Keepers, have been emboldened to come out proudly to display their hate.

In Canada, while we might not have had incidents such as the January 6, 2021, assault on the Capitol, we have much to confront and deal with too. Barbara Perry is the director of the Centre on Hate, Bias and Extremism with Ontario Tech University. In a 2015 study funded by Public Safety Canada, she identified more than 100 active far-right groups in Canada. A year into a sequel to this study, she said that number had jumped to almost 300. In a Labour Day, 2020, interview with the Ontario Federation of Labour, Perry said that the demographics of far-right groups are shifting, becoming a movement of middle-aged adults, often well-educated and holding middle-class jobs.

Perry reports that hate crimes are rising at an alarming rate. Most victims are Jews and Muslims, with incidents against Indigenous Peoples stronger in certain cities and regions. B'Nai Brith reports a steady increase in online anti-Semitism since 2018, with over 2,000 incidents in 2020. The COVID-19 crisis has seen a dramatic increase in anti-Asian racial harassment, both physical and online, as many people blame the outbreak on China. Hate crimes against members of the Asian community in Vancouver spiked by 878% in 2020 over 2019, according to CTV News.

A December 2020 report by Boston Consulting Group and CivicAction, a Toronto civil society organization,

Paul Moist

Paul Moist served as national president of the Canadian Union of Public Employees for 12 years and is a lifelong activist. Paul is one of the great labour leaders in Canada.

Where do you find hope?

"My 40 years of labour activism were grounded in both core labour beliefs and the hope for a better world for all.

"Nelson Mandela said, 'May your choices reflect your hopes, not your fears.' Wise words for a life on the left. I learned early on that organized labour had much to learn from progressive groups outside the labour movement in common pursuit of social justice for all.

"While unions perform a key democratic role in pursuit of economic and workplace rights for workers, we seek those very goals for all citizens, and we know that none of us are truly free so long as others are marginalized and denied basic human rights.

"Collective agreements for workers are important, so too is the social contract that strives for justice for all citizens. This can only be achieved by broad coalitions of progressive citizens, united in common cause.

"The collective pursuit of social justice for all is a never-ending journey, which reminds me of the instructive words of Eleanor Roosevelt, who said, 'Surely, in the light of history, it is more intelligent to hope rather than fear, to try rather than not to try.'"

found that anti-Black racism in Canada is pervasive. For example, Black students are four times more likely to be expelled from a Toronto high school than white students, and Black university graduates earn only 80 cents for every dollar earned by white university graduates, despite having the same credentials.

And the frontlines of our "mighty contests" for water and climate justice are most often poor or racialized communities. The term environmental racism refers to environmental injustice that is tied to minority communities. All over the world, the pollution from extractive industry is at its worst in poor communities that are often Indigenous, often racialized, places where the people traditionally have had limited power. Racialized communities are disproportionately burdened with health hazards through policies and practices that force them to live in proximity to sources of toxic waste, such as sewage works, landfills, power stations and oil refineries. Many wealthy countries export their waste to poorer countries, where it ends up in already disadvantaged communities.

Even progressive civil society organizations have to confront institutionalized racism. We must be aware of this reality and seek out ways to connect with and support the struggles of racialized and Indigenous peoples. But progressive activist groups must be careful that in recognizing what some call identity politics, we don't break down into silos that further division rather than inclusion. We mustn't ask racialized communities to give up their fight for justice to a "greater" social goal, but incorporate their lived reality into those larger struggles in a meaningful way, using identity as a bridge, not a wall.

It is also okay to admit that differences may remain unresolved and that is part of the process. As longtime ecologist and activist Rex Weyler wrote in a November 2021 message to young people on the Greenpeace website, we build deep diversity by abstaining from superficial virtue signalling and abandoning the expectation that all dispute or controversy can be resolved. "Part of quieting our ego is the work of shedding the desire to be correct, or to make others wrong. Building deep diversity is the art of being at peace with multiple opinions, holding contradictory ideas and ideals in our consciousness with patience and compassion."

Because the lack of water disproportionately impacts Indigenous and racialized communities, their leadership is crucial to any campaigns we undertake. Their reality and analysis have to be the basis for the work ahead. Coming together to fight for universal water rights, for example, builds a larger movement and leads to laws, that, while they are meant to apply to all, are most crucial for the poor, marginalized and minority communities. Successfully ending water shut-offs, for instance, may on paper apply to all, but in reality, it means the most to those who have been without water services.

Even progressive civil society organizations have to confront institutionalized racism.

The people of Detroit know this. Welfare rights and anti-poverty groups, environmentalists, labour unions and many others joined the Black community in fighting for their right to water. Detroit Jews for Justice put their involvement this way: "The slow work of building relationships is at the heart of building a collective. We honour the tensions, frustrations and intensity of building community. It is only through being rooted in a strong community that we can have strong relationships with others. We believe our work is most meaningful and effective when we struggle against the injustices that are right in front of us and impact those around us."

Monica Lewis-Patrick, civil rights veteran and president of We the People of Detroit, said, "Detroit Jews for Justice has been an intentional partner in building a collective of resistance and restorative justice for Detroiters on issues like water, housing, police brutality, and many of the anti-democratic policies that are being used against the citizens. Gratitude and Solidarity!"

This gives me hope not just for the immediate goal of housing, pay and water but for building the kinds of community and democracy that are the only antidote to the hatred of the New Right.

Serve the oppressed and the grassroots

The work we do must serve those who are the victims of water and climate injustice. Do not mistake me, this is not about noblesse oblige. This is about being willing to share and bear witness to others' pain and suffering and allowing ourselves to care at that deeper level. The struggles that stand out for me are always the ones where I met the community directly and became enraged on their behalf. That rage would fuel me a long time afterward.

One such experience was a trip to Guatemala in 2011 to meet with victims of brutality connected to foreign mining companies poisoning local water sources with cyanide by-product. There, I met a young man in a wheelchair, his spine severed by a bullet from pro-mining thugs who had terrorized his village. I met a woman who had been gang-raped by men who killed her husband. I met an elderly woman who would not sell her property to the mining company so they turned her water off. When that didn't scare her away, a man hiding behind a tree outside her small dwelling shot her in the face, leaving her for dead. The police refused to take her to the hospital so her frantic daughter had to take her mother in a taxi. The woman miraculously survived and still would not back down.

This community launched lawsuits in the mining companies' own countries, and one is still being fought out in a Toronto court as Hudbay, one of the companies involved, is Canadian. Grahame Russell of Rights Action, who brought me to Guatemala and who has been tireless in his defence of this community, explains in a newsletter, "Every now and then there is a human rights/territory/environmental defence struggle that breaks through the thick walls of global corporate corruption and impunity. The Hudbay lawsuits begin to get to the heart of how the unjust global economic order often works. Extraordinarily, 13 exploited and impoverished, violently evicted, raped and shot at Indigenous people from a remote corner of a distant country (Guatemala) have brought their mining company accountability struggle to the home country (Canada) and city (Toronto) of a powerful global company.

They have brought their justice struggle to the corridors of wealth and power in the global mining industry."

Not all the people and communities who are in life-and-death struggles over the climate crisis and the lack of clean water live in poor countries. Remembering who we serve in this work keeps us rooted in their struggles and clear in our commitment. When Berlin became a Blue Community and pledged to honour the human right to water and sanitation, it funded a waterless toilet project — small, clean, private wooden shelters that use sawdust and hand sanitizers instead of water — to provide sanitation services to those in need. They are now set up in the red-light districts so sex workers can have a safe place to use a bathroom and for the many thousands of homeless and migrants living in city parks and under thoroughfares. It is only one step in the long march for justice, but an important one.

Be kind to yourself and others

Mark Twain said that kindness is the language the deaf can hear and the blind can see. I cannot emphasize strongly enough how important I think this is.

In their 2010 book, *On Kindness*, psychoanalyst Adam Phillips and historian Barbara Taylor write that kindness has become a "forbidden pleasure" in today's Western culture of competition, personal status and self-protection. Outside of one's family, they say, kindness — which they define as the ability to bear the vulnerability of others and therefore of oneself — has become a sign of weakness. In fact, expressing hate for people with other views has become an ugly part of current culture. (Anyone who has experienced trolls and anonymous attacks on social media can attest to how terrifying and demoralizing it can be.) If we think of humans as essentially competitive, as we are encouraged to do, say the authors, then kindness looks distinctly old-fashioned, indeed nostalgic — a vestige from another time.

But despite our resistance to kindness as a societal value, kindness being the "saboteur of the successful life," Phillips and Taylor say that there is nothing we feel more constantly deprived of than kindness. "The kind life — the life lived in instinctive sympathetic identification with the vulnerabilities and attractions of others — is the life we are more inclined to live, and indeed is the one we are often living without letting ourselves know that this is what we are doing. People are leading secretly kind lives all the time but without a language in which to express this, or cultural support for it. . . . We need to know how we have come to believe that the best lives we can lead seem to involve sacrificing the best things about ourselves; and how we have come to believe that there are pleasures greater than kindness."

The culture of competition and judgment exists on the left as well as the right. I have seen and experienced too many examples of progressive groups and individuals working for justice turning on one another. We must learn to be more tolerant of our colleagues and gentle in our dealings. I am not talking about papering over political differences, but there is always room for courtesy.

Martin Luther King Jr. said, "We are caught in an inescapable network of mutuality, tied in a single garment of destiny. Whatever affects one, directly affects all indirectly." This is true for the Earth and ecosystems; it is also true for movements. A nasty remark, a flash of anger, a poison drop of gossip, all lead to distrust and affect our work. We must find ways to air grievances and differences in a respectful way. Take time to say thank you. Acknowledge and give credit for the good work of others. Be there for allies in their struggles. Let them know you care how they are. Be kind.

I have found that it is important for the morale of an organization to take the time to socialize — playing baseball, sharing a meal, going for a walk, having a beer. This is also true for boards whose members often go unappreciated and are often distrusted by staff for whom a board can be a convenient scapegoat. Board members are volunteers who work hard and often don't get recognition for the behind-the-scenes work they do. Making board meetings as pleasant as possible and building in downtime is really important for morale. As is kindness.

There is always room for courtesy.

Be kind to yourself as well. Take time for yourself. Keep good health practices. Allow yourself to be tired and discouraged and turn to those who care to help you through. Step away when you feel overwhelmed. Set limits on what you will expose yourself to. It is crucial to be open to valid criticism, but you don't have to expose yourself to abuse and you owe no one to take it. Bernice King, American minister and daughter of Martin Luther King Jr. and Coretta Scott King, wrote on Twitter, "I don't have to respond whenever provoked. No one does. Steward your energy well. We have justice work to do. And strategy to outline. And self-care to prioritize. And love to live. It's okay to let provocateurs leave empty handed."

Learn to recognize and deal with burnout — your own and others'. Emma Lui is a water activist living in Quebec who has both studied and experienced burnout. She says even when you find your work rewarding, you can experience burnout. Symptoms can include exhaustion, insomnia, anxiety, depression, illness, pain, the inability to concentrate and emotions such as despair, grief, anger, resentment, sadness, guilt, shame and compassion fatigue. Burnout can result from working hard and caring deeply, but it can also come from internalizing the very systems we are fighting, such as capitalism, colonialism, racism, violence and the destruction of nature. Workplace trauma can be devastating and have serious side effects on one's health.

What we see as activists, such as the suffering of others, is very hard and leaves many feeling guilty if we nurture ourselves or rest or have fun. Noting that healing is justice, Lui writes on Rabble.ca, "Honouring the needs *Be kind to yourself as well. Take time for yourself.* and cycles of our bodies in the same way we call for the honouring of lands, waters, ecosystems, wildlife, people and the other things we fight to protect is critical to justice work."

She shares her advice on how organizations can identify and address burnout:

- "Structure work cycles to be regenerative." This includes nourishment, celebration, sharing stories, debriefing, processing grief, resting, reflecting and dreaming new visions after an action or event.

- "Carve out spaces for people to step back from the work." Structuring groups and organizations in ways that allow and encourage members or staff to step back to restore, reflect and heal will allow them to come back healthier and more whole.
- "Integrate community care." We have a tendency to blame ourselves when we experience burnout. Just as it takes a village to raise a child, it takes a community to offer love and support to friends and co-workers in the movement when they are suffering.
- "Provide on-site trauma response support and care at direct actions, marches and events." Lui reminds us that confronting power at a blockade or protest march or even before a committee of elected officials can trigger anxiety and fear, especially for minority groups who have experienced violence and discrimination. Healing and addressing burnout is the missing piece that will enable our movements to continue our work in a regenerative way. Healing is integral to building a society based on justice, equity, health and compassion.

Healing and kindness are the path to hope. The great American author Henry James said, "Three things in life are important. The first is to be kind. The second is to be kind. The third is to be kind."

CHAPTER FIVE

THE NEXT STEPS TO TAKE

Let us postpone our pessimism for better times.

EDUARDO GALEANO

I n the aftermath of the Battle of Seattle, Paul Hawken, American social entrepreneur, environmentalist and author, wrote a brilliant essay in the *Sun Magazine* about what he saw and experienced that week. Time, he wrote, can be measured differently depending on how it is defined. The dominant time frame of economic globalization is commercial. Businesses must be quick and grow at an ever-faster rate or they will be "punished, pummeled and bankrupted." For corporations to survive, everything must speed up — transportation, information and technology. A second time frame is culture, which moves more slowly, rooted as it is in the historical templates of tradition, family, faith, community and identity.

The third and slowest chronology, says Hawken, is "earth, nature, the web of life." As ephemeral as it may seem, it is the slowest clock, always ticking, always there, responding to "long, ancient evolutionary cycles that are beyond civilization." These three chronologies conflict and languages, cultures, forests and fisheries are extirpated in the name of speeding up business. Hawken argues that what happened on the streets of Seattle in 1999 at the WTO ministerial was that quick time met slow time and that everything the power-brokers of the WTO thought they had left behind — he calls it the "shadow world" — strode into the halls of power and claimed its place. All these years later, in his assertion that we destroy culture and nature in the name of "progress," Paul Hawken has been proven right.

The age of nature

To survive the climate crisis, we must look to the Indigenous practice of long-term thinking and seventh-generation decision-making. In a January 2021 CBC story, Rick Hill, member of the Tuscarora Six Nations of southern Ontario, echoes Paul Hawken's caution about the clashes of chronology. If you think seven generations ahead, Hill says, you have to go slow and take care. "We're stuck with this idea that growth is necessary in order to be modern, to be competitive in the world . . . [Indigenous people] may be out of step with modern society. But we say modern society is out of step with the Earth."

In his 2020 book, *The Good Ancestor: A Radical Prescription for Long-Term Thinking*, British philosopher Roman Krznaric calls on us to shift our perspective of instant gratification to what he calls "deep-time humility" and live our lives with our grandchildren's grandchildren in mind. Krznaric says that to be a good ancestor, we have to achieve sustainability in our own lives and lifetime. He gives examples of some cities making 100-year sustainability plans and notes, like Hawken, "a recognition of the need to extend our time horizons."

Sheila Watt-Cloutier is an Inuk from northern Quebec and a highly regarded human- and Indigenous-rights advocate. In a February 2021 interview for the *Globe and Mail*, she described how the climate crisis has affected life for her people. It endangers "more than polar bears," she says, it threatens communities trying to survive on the ice and land to maintain a more traditional, holistic way of life. She calls for a recognition of how closely the environment, health, economics, culture and rights are linked.

To survive the climate crisis, we must look to the Indigenous practice of long-term thinking and seventh-generation decision-making.

"The Earth is a living, breathing entity just the same as our bodies are. Our survival utterly depends on living in nature, not apart from it. In addressing climate change, we need to move away from focusing solely on the language of economics, which further adds to the destruction of our atmosphere, our land, our waters, and wildlife, and we need to emphasize and consider the impact on human life and rights as well. Climate change is very much about a moral and ethical imperative."

Our modern society is out of step with the Earth. Our survival utterly depends on living in nature, not apart from it. Both Hill and Watt-Cloutier offer the key to a liveable future. The time has come for the age of nature. I am not going to repeat the terrifying statistics on the multiple threats to our planet from global warming, rising oceans, fires and drought. We are all living with them. What I do believe with all my heart is that humans are ready to embrace a new relationship with the Earth and the other beings with which we share it. Thankfully, David Suzuki tells us that it is not too late: "Work with nature and it will be more forgiving than we deserve."

What I do believe with all my heart is that humans are ready to embrace a new relationship with the Earth and the other beings with which we share it.

Climate activist Bill McKibben says that things happen slowly and then begin to gain momentum. This was a lesson I learned from American activist-educator Bill Moyer, who, in 1987, wrote the "movement bible" called the Movement Action Plan. He believed that movements failed because people gave up too soon, feeling their efforts were futile in the face of powerful institutions, often just before they were about to succeed. So he laid out the stages movements must go through to succeed. Australian youth climate activist Anna Rose offers a précis of Moyer's movement stages on the website of an Australian Commons library.

At the first stage, people recognize that there are violations and injustices but are quiet. Then as they see that their governments and institutions are failing to address these violations, they start to mobilize. However, "takeoff" of a movement requires preconditions that build up over many years. When it happens, and a grassroots movement bursts into the public spotlight, a previously unrecognized social or environmental problem becomes an issue many are talking about. Often this stage is attended by a "trigger event" followed by an action campaign that includes large rallies and civil disobedience.

The next stage is a make-or-break one, and requires mobilizing widespread public support. The objective is a transformation from spontaneous protest operating in a short-term crisis framework to a long-term struggle to achieve positive change. This stage must win over the sympathies, opinions and support of a majority of the populace to create a new social and political consensus. The new social consensus turns the tide of power against the old powerholders, beginning an endgame process that leads to the movement's ultimate success. Moyer didn't end his stages there, however, but advised that any victory is not the end of the struggle but a basis for continuing it and creating new beginnings.

Although there are terrible environmental violations taking place in many parts of the world, I believe that humanity is reaching this stage of popular agreement on both the nature of the crisis and its solutions. We are finally ready to create a new relationship with nature.

Part of my optimism comes from young people and their teachers. I know I wrote earlier that they are feeling overwhelmed and frightened for the future. They aren't sheltered from the reality of what we are facing. But that really is informing a whole generation of the crises we face and encouraging them to help us find solutions. I work a lot with young people and cannot believe how knowledgeable and savvy they are about the climate crisis and the environment and how committed they are to creating a more just and equitable world. When enough of the population has internalized certain knowledge and values, we can change. Look at what's happened for women in just one century.

Hopeful signs for the climate

There are many reasons for some optimism. In February 2021, the journal *Nature* published several scientific studies showing the ozone layer is healing after recent setbacks. In 1987, the Montreal Protocol — a global agreement to protect the stratospheric ozone layer by phasing out CFC chemicals — was signed, leading to a steady decline in their manufacture and use. But atmospheric measurements in 2018 pointed to illegal CFC production in eastern China, which appears to have been addressed. The scientists report that the ozone layer is once again anticipated to recover by mid-century.

When enough of the population has internalized certain knowledge and values, we can change.

While most countries in the world are not yet on track to meet their Paris or Glasgow COP commitments, there are some promising signs. In September 2021, E3G, a European climate think tank, reported that more than three-quarters of the world's planned coal plants have been scrapped since the 2015 climate agreement and that 40 countries no longer have any future coal power plants. At COP26, more than 40 countries, including Canada, agreed to phase out coal-fired power altogether. Another sign of hope is that the United States rejoined the Paris pact when Joe Biden became president and pledged to take action on the climate crisis. At COP26, the US joined the European Union, UK, Canada and other countries in announcing it will achieve net-zero carbon emissions by 2050. As well, the US and Canada were among 20 countries that committed to stop financing all fossil fuels abroad, a move widely applauded by environmental groups.

Many climate activists were deeply disappointed with the final outcome of COP26. They rightly pointed out that the concept of "net zero emissions" instead of ending fossil fuel production altogether still allows the burning of fossil fuels. They were also rightly critical that wealthy countries can continue to pollute by using carbon and forest offsets, buying up land or planting trees in the Global South in the name of conservation. One called it the worst land grabbing COP in history, saying there is not enough land or forests in the world to take in the carbon still permitted by the deal. But others pointed out that this was the first COP to even use the term "fossil fuels" in its final declaration and hailed the creation of a new nation state alliance to control their actual production. And a new and unexpected pact between China and the US to work together on cutting emissions was broadly welcomed by leaders and climate activists alike.

Importantly, India, the world's third largest carbon emitter, pledged to hit net-zero emissions by 2070. Admittedly, this is decades later than many other countries; but it marks the first time India has put an end date on its contribution to the climate crisis, noted many observers. University of Oxford political scientist Thomas Hale said with his breakthrough, countries representing 90% of global GDP are now covered by a net-zero target. While China made no new commitments in its letter to COP26, months earlier, it too made its first concrete commitment, promising to hit peak emissions before 2030 and move to full carbon neutrality by 2060. Ma Jun, director of the Beijing-based NGO Institute of Public & Environmental Affairs, explained China's importance to this issue in a September 2019 interview with *Time*. Because China is the world's most populous country and the largest emitter of carbon, Ma Jun said, if it can meet its vast potential for emissions reduction, it will play an enormous role in tackling the climate crisis.

He points to the fact that after suffering severe smog in 2011, the product of rising coal consumption, the Chinese government initiated a national action plan that slowed the growth of coal consumption, resulting in improved air quality and lower emissions. In fact, a team of researchers has found that China is on a trajectory to hit peak emissions earlier than 2030. Their analysis, published in a July 2019 edition of *Nature Sustainability*, cited the reduction in the use of coal as well as the fact that as Chinese cities become richer, their emissions per capita begin to decline. Ma Jun reminds us that because China manufactures products for global supply chains, its carbon footprint is really a shared global burden.

(It is difficult to verify the reports of improved environmental practices in China and other countries that control the media and public communication. Other reports cite new coal plants being built in China as I write. As well, I do not intend my words of hope for a climate commitment to blunt criticism of human rights abuses in China or elsewhere. Nevertheless, the international community was heartened to hear of this climate commitment from the Chinese government after so many years of waiting.)

A study that took place between 2016 and 2019 found that global commitments to curb greenhouse gas emissions are working. Published in March 2021 in *Nature Climate Change*, it reported that regulations to curb emissions in 64 countries — including most wealthy nations and one-third of the middle-income ones — slashed roughly 160 million metric tons of carbon dioxide per year, thanks to some 2,000 new climate laws worldwide. Many hope a similar agreement on another serious contributor to the climate crisis can see similar effects. Methane gas is a by product of much human activity, including industrial agriculture, landfills and natural gas production and is many times more potent than CO_2. At COP26, more than 100 countries signed the Global Methane Pledge to limit methane emissions by 30% compared to 2020 levels.

Perhaps the greatest sign of hope is the growing understanding of nature-based solutions to the climate crisis.

Early summer 2021 saw four important milestones in the quest to slow climate chaos. In a move that surprised many, the G7 countries pledged to end their financial support for coal development overseas — a major step toward phasing out this particularly dirty fossil fuel. Poland announced its intention to close Europe's most polluting power plant, the coal-fired Belchatów plant, by 2036, using money from the EU's Just Transition Fund.

The International Energy Agency said that all new development of fossil fuels must end within a year to give the world the chance of meeting its climate commitment of 1.5°C. And in a case brought forward by Friends of the Earth, a Dutch court ordered Shell Oil to cut its emission 45% by 2030 to be in line with the goals of the Paris Climate Agreement. Huge signs of hope.

Ecosystem Restoration

Perhaps the greatest sign of hope is the growing understanding that ecosystem restoration — also called nature-based solutions — is crucial to the climate crisis. While many governments and scientists around the world are working to wean us off fossil fuels and support alternative and sustainable energy sources, there is a tsunami of interest in how the protection and restoration of forests, soils, watersheds and wetlands can help us mitigate the climate crisis.

In 2017, a study published in the *Proceedings of the National Academy of Sciences* found that the simple act of preserving existing forests, wetlands and grasslands could provide more than one-third of the emissions reductions needed to stabilize global temperature by 2°C by 2030. Three years later, scientists from a dozen countries went further, saying that, in addition to protecting existing natural landscapes, we need to restore damaged ones and rewild some of our cultivated land as well. Their report, *Global Priority Areas for Ecosystem Restoration*, was published in an October 2020 edition of *Nature*. The scientists found that restoring natural landscapes damaged by human exploitation can be one of the most effective and inexpensive ways to combat the climate crisis while also boosting dwindling wildlife populations. "We find restoring 15% of converted lands in priority areas could avoid 60% of expected extinctions while sequestering 299 gigatonnes of CO_2 — 30% of the total CO_2 increase in the atmosphere since the Industrial Revolution," they said. This study shows that ecosystem restoration needs far more attention — and funding — than they have had in the past. And governments are finally listening.

In preparation for a 2021 world summit on post-COVID recovery, more than 60 countries pledged to place wildlife protection and climate commitment at the heart of post-pandemic recovery. According to *The Guardian*, all signatories to a September 2020 Leaders' Pledge for Nature promised to clamp down on pollution, embrace sustainable economic systems and eliminate the dumping of plastics in oceans by the middle of the century. Their ten-point plan seeks to reduce deforestation, halt unsustainable fishing practices, eliminate environmentally harmful subsidies and begin the transition to sustainable food production systems. "Science clearly shows that biodiversity loss, land and ocean degradation, pollution, resource depletion and climate change are accelerating at an unprecedented rate . . . A transformative change is needed: we cannot simply carry on as before," said the leaders, including those from France, Germany, Canada, Great Britain, Bangladesh, Colombia and Mexico.

In September 2020, Great Britain, the EU and Canada pledged to protect 30% of their land by 2030. A month later, at a UN summit aimed at galvanizing action to protect wildlife, famed British environmental broadcaster Sir David Attenborough launched a campaign by 130 conservation groups for the world to invest US$500 billion a year to halt the destruction of nature. Only about 1% of the finance devoted to the climate crisis now goes to nature restoration. He told delegates that climate funding should be put in the hands of locally led conservation groups.

Then in February 2021, United Nations secretary-general António Guterres published the findings of a major United Nations Environment Programme report that recommended redirecting more than US$5 trillion in annual subsidies that now go to the fossil fuel industry, industrial agriculture, fishing and mining. This will accelerate a shift to a low-carbon future and aid the restoration of ecosystems. Noting that the war humanity is waging on nature can be seen in human suffering, towering economic losses and the acceleration of the erosion of life on Earth, the report, *Making Peace with Nature*, said that governments must look beyond economic growth as the sole indicator of performance and give priority to the preservation of ecosystems. This is a huge step forward.

On June 6, 2021, the United Nations General Assembly officially launched the UN Decade for Ecosystem Restoration at a Rome meeting of world, faith-based and environmental leaders. They released a report saying humans are using about 1.6 times the resources that nature can sustainably renew every year and said the revival of ecosystems must be met with all the ambition of the space race. Food and Agriculture Organization director-general Qu Dongyu called for a massive global movement to save the planet's terrestrial and marine ecosystems. "Business as usual is not an option. We need to prevent, halt, and reverse the degradation of ecosystems worldwide, including our farmlands and forests, our rivers and oceans." UN General Assembly president Volkan Bozkir said that restoring nature is the "test of our generation."

Here I want to issue a caution. Some business leaders and neoliberal politicians have adopted nature-based solutions as a way to divert public money to private enterprise through market-based solutions to the environmental crisis. They call nature "natural capital" or "natural assets" and put a dollar figure on the "services" nature provides. They seek to "protect" nature by bringing it into the market economy where it would have to abide by market rules. Like carbon-trading, corporations could "offset" their threat to biodiversity by buying or trading the right to continue polluting practices while governments continue to deregulate. This important new consensus to base our most urgent policies on protecting nature must not be hijacked for private profit.

Restoration of nature is already happening

An alliance has formed to promote natural landscapes across Europe. Rewilding Europe aims to rewild one million hectares of land, creating ten wildlife and wilderness areas across the continent. Bison have been successfully reintroduced in the Netherlands and Romania. Water buffalo have been reintroduced to the Danube Delta, the largest wetland in Europe. Germany has recovered a huge mass of land in Lusatia destroyed by a century and a half of coal mining, creating 24 artificial lakes, marinas, beaches, parks and wildlife refuges. Birds and aquatic life have returned to the area. A plan in Scotland would rec-reate partial forest cover right across the land and beavers have been reintroduced to the River Tay. The 100-hectare Grand Barry nature reserve in southeast France is under-taking one of the largest rewilding experiments anywhere, banning hunting, fishing, logging, farming and the use of motor vehicles in order to let nature recover unaided and unobstructed by people.

And people are finally paying attention to the oceans. Following a decade of discussions, UN negotiations were launched in 2018 for a legally binding treaty to protect biodiversity on the high seas, those marine areas outside of national jurisdictions.

Elin Kelsey writes in *Hope Matters* that in 2000 only 0.7% of the world's oceans were designated as marine protected areas (MPAs). Kelsey wrote a scientific brief for the creation of one of the first, the Mariana Trench, located within US territorial waters off the Pacific coast. Since then, this MPA has been surpassed by many others. Twenty-four countries and the European Union created the world's largest marine sanctuary in Antarctica's Ross Sea in 2016, and now 8% of the oceans are designated as marine protected areas. Kelsey reports that these sanc-tuaries are reversing degradation and rebuilding ocean life. In 2020, Great Britain, Canada and the EU pledged to protect 30% of their territorial seas by 2030. And in May 2021, Australia moved to create two major new marine protected areas that cover an expanse of ocean twice the size of the Great Barrier Reef Marine Park.

And there was an exciting breakthrough at the world congress of the International Union for the Conservation of Nature held in Marseille France in September 2021, when governments, NGOs and civil society groups overwhelmingly voted in favour of a moratorium on deep-sea mineral mining. Scientists and environmental groups warn that a deep-sea mining free-for-all would disturb ecosystems and food sources, leading to toxic spills and the loss of entire marine species.

Another powerful movement is promoting the protection of existing forests and the restoration of forests by the planting of billions of trees. Scientists estimate that the planet has about half the trees it had before the rise of human civilization and that reforestation will help restore hydrologic cycles and create carbon sinks. At COP26, over 100 countries and the European Union announced over US $19 billion in public and private funds to halt and reverse deforestation by 2030. While many are sceptical that countries such as Russia and Brazil signed the pact given their terrible record of forest destruction, others welcomed an opportunity to influence them toward global goals. Importantly, at least US $1.7 billion will be given to Indigenous Peoples and local communities in the Global South in recognition of their key role in protecting the planet's lands and forests. There are very real concerns that some plans for conservation and biodiversity restoration are leading to displacement or harm of the local people. It is also vital that trees are planted for long term restoration with the direct involvement of local communities and not as for-profit plantations.

There are exciting projects already underway: the Bonn Challenge is a global campaign by the International Union of Concerned Scientists to restore and reforest 350 million hectares by 2030. And in May 2020, the European Union pledged to plant three billion trees and expand organic farming exponentially by 2030. The European Commission, in announcing this plan, tied it to avoiding future pandemics like the COVID-19 crisis. By protecting habitats and limiting human interaction with wild species, we can limit animal-to-human infection transfer.

In December 2020, Canadian prime minister Justin Trudeau announced Canada's plan to plant two billion trees over ten years. Then environment minister Jonathan Wilkinson said, "We have both the responsibility and the opportunity. We have the second largest land mass, a fifth of the world's freshwater and the longest coastline in the world that together are critical for biodiversity and securing carbon in nature in the fight against climate change."

Coming under fire for the destruction of the boreal forest, provincial and federal governments are stepping up to protect Canada's natural heritage. Alberta has recently announced plans to create the largest contiguous boreal forest area in the world with an expansion of the Kitaskino Nuwenëné Wildland in the northeast of the province and the Canadian government created the Thaidene Nëné National Park Reserve covering over two and a half million hectares of lakes, old-growth boreal forests, rivers and wildlife habitat in the Northwest Territories. In both cases, local Indigenous communities have been partners in the planning.

The Great Green Wall is a multi-country project in Africa to plant 8,000 kilometres of trees and plants across the width of the continent. Launched in the late 1990s, it is already bringing back life to some of Africa's degraded landscapes, providing food security, jobs and a reason for people to stay on the land. Once complete, the Great Green Wall will be the largest living structure on the planet. In just one day, July 29, 2019, Ethiopians planted 350 million seedlings.

These and similar projects are paying off. In a May 2021 report, the World Wildlife Fund said that since 2020 the world has already regrown enough forest to cover France — nearly 59 million hectares — capable of soaking up and storing 5.9 gigatonnes of carbon dioxide, more than the annual emissions of the entire US.

The United States under Joe Biden has become a beacon of hope after the destructive environmental decisions of the Trump administration. President Biden has paused oil and gas drilling on federal lands and offshore waters for review, eliminated fossil fuel subsidies and will transform the government's vast fleet of cars and trucks into electric vehicles. He said that millions of well-paid jobs will flow from investments in clean energy, from the implementation of energy-efficient measures for homes and from the cleanup of derelict oil wells. Biden has set up an office of domestic climate policy in the White

House and pledged to set a new goal of conserving 30% of American land and oceans by 2030.

We all watch the terrible destruction of the Amazon of Brazil with despair. But there are exciting initiatives taking place in Latin America. In 2018, the Inter-American Court recognized the fundamental right to a healthy environment. In April 2021, the United Nations released a major report arguing that Indigenous and tribal communities in Latin America and the Caribbean are not only the most harmed by the climate crisis and other environmental disasters, but are the guardians of the region's forests whose leadership must be recognized in the fight against climate change. Their territories contain a third of the carbon stored in the forests of the region, and Indigenous communities protect these lands and forests, practising ancestral ways that must be respected and protected in law, said the UN.

That same month, 12 Latin American countries ratified the Escazú Agreement, the first environmental treaty of the region, guaranteeing "the full and effective implementation of the rights of access to environmental information, public participation and access to justice" for their people. Latin America is the most dangerous region in the world for environmental defenders, so it is particularly important that the treaty pledges support for environmental and human rights defenders by codifying their right to protest. International civil rights network CIVICUS praised the agreement and urged remaining Latin American countries to join. "Escazú is the hope that change is possible for Latin America. It is a triumph for communities and civil society."

Much hope also lies in the innovative policies and practices of cities. In his 2020 book, *Solved: How the World's Great Cities Are Fixing the Climate Crisis*, former Toronto mayor David Miller says that municipalities are playing a largely unnoticed but crucial role in fighting the climate crisis. Cities are nimbler and can adapt more quickly to the demands of residents. They retrofit old buildings and regulate the construction of new buildings for energy efficiency. They save water by fixing leaking pipes. They build parks and gardens, plant trees, promote public transportation, create bike lanes and implement best practices for solid waste management. In fact, Miller says, some cities are so advanced, they are even exceeding the Paris Agreement their national governments have signed.

Civil society steps up

None of these promises will mean anything if governments are not held accountable by their citizens. This is why civil action for social and environmental justice matters more than ever.

There are several central themes guiding the politics of our time. One is the understanding that governments of all political stripes have failed to stop climate chaos and environmental devastation. This isn't to say there is no difference between political parties. But the neoliberal policies of the Thatcher/Reagan years were picked up by liberal politicians of Western democracies claiming it was possible to be both "socially progressive" and "fiscally conservative." Selling themselves as progressives who cared about inequality and poverty, they enthusiastically adopted the core tenets of economic globalization and the promise that they would provide opportunity for all. In the UK, Labour leader Tony Blair called it the "Third Way." Bill Clinton and Barack Obama embraced free trade and worked closely with their big business sectors in setting policy, as did Canadian Liberal governments under Jean Chrétien and Paul Martin. But of course, without the concurrent investments in social security and education, they abandoned their people to unbridled global market forces, which in turn set the stage for the rise of right-wing populism.

None of these promises will mean anything if governments are not held accountable by their citizens.

Now activists are fighting for a new form of democracy where governments are guided by projects coming from local communities, environmental and social justice movements, and the grassroots. The best successes in climate crisis policy, for example, have come from well-organized civil society movements. Concerted and coordinated opposition, consisting of a coalition of groups and individuals, stopped the proposed Energy East pipeline in Canada. This pipeline would have carried Alberta bitumen — the dirtiest oil on Earth, laced with chemicals to facilitate its flow through the pipes — to the east coast of Canada to be put on tankers and shipped to refineries in Texas or across the ocean to Europe. It was the largest pipeline ever proposed for North America and would have crossed over 3,000 waterways, including the St. Lawrence River. Cross-border grassroots resistance also stopped the "unstoppable" Keystone pipeline that would have endangered 1,073 waterways in Montana, South Dakota and Nebraska. Other citizen-led movements using occupations, marches and court challenges have held up the building of the Trans Mountain pipeline in Canada and a new Line 3 pipeline from Alberta to Wisconsin.

Over the course of several years, I spoke on the issue to packed crowds in dozens of towns and cities along the Energy East pipeline's path and can attest to the passion in those communities for the protection of their water. I attended a number of Bill McKibben's protests against the Keystone Pipeline at the White House and was arrested at a demonstration on Parliament Hill in September 2011. The people I met in the course of this campaign convinced me that we would eventually win this struggle.

The Green New Deal — a bold plan to decarbonize the US economy by 2050 while creating jobs and reducing economic inequality — is another example of transformation from below. While the concept wasn't new, the youth-led Sunrise Movement brought it to national attention during an occupation of incoming house speaker Nancy Pelosi's office in 2018. In 2019, NYC congresswoman Alexandria Ocasio-Cortez and Massachusetts senator Ed Markey released a formal House resolution, which was not adopted, but its principles continue to be championed by groups such as Sunrise Movement, 350.org, Food & Water Watch, Jane Fonda's Fire-Drill Fridays, the youth-led Fridays for Future and, now, most of the Democratic Party. Responding to a powerful civil society climate movement, the European Commission launched the European Green Deal in 2019, with the goal of making Europe carbon neutral by 2050. It was adopted by European Parliament in 2020.

In Canada, the Pact for a Green New Deal has brought together a wide range of civil society organizations and grassroots movements of workers, environmentalists, students, artists, Indigenous leaders and scientists, and is being heard by all levels of government. Greenpeace lays out three steps necessary to successfully adopt a green agenda: unite a diverse movement; develop a shared vision; and push political leaders to act.

A guiding principle of the politics of our time must be that the solution to the climate crisis and other environmental threats be viewed through the lens of social and environmental justice. It cannot be tackled in isolation. Not only are Indigenous and racialized people more likely to live in communities exposed to the worst forms of pollution, they are often the first victims when industrial pollution causes health problems. They are also more likely to live in poverty. In many countries, that means inferior, or no, access to clean water, health care or social services. Climate impacts can exacerbate existing inequitable social conditions. President Biden has shown he understands this issue, and in his April 2021 budget, he earmarked US$1.4 billion for environmental justice initiatives.

Climate justice recognizes that we are not all equally responsible for the current crisis. Some countries, corporations and elites create, per capita, most of the annual greenhouse gas emissions but escape its worst effects.

Privileged people can buy their way into gated communities and live in wealthy suburbs where the air is clean and the water pure. The UN says the impacts of the climate crisis will not be borne equally or fairly between rich and poor, women and men, and older and younger generations. As is always the case, says UN Secretary-General Guterres, the poor and vulnerable are the first to suffer and the worst hit.

To tackle the climate crisis, we need to tackle poverty, racism and injustice. That means working closely with impacted groups and communities and taking their lead on solutions. We need the experience and expertise of those most affected. I think here of the Inuit and other communities of the far north who gather vital information on the changes in ice cover, the behaviour of wildlife and the changing weather patterns that the climate crisis has wrought on their land. Fortunately, awareness of this need to seek climate justice is taking root everywhere.

A guiding principle of the politics of our time must be that the solution to the climate crisis and other environmental threats be viewed through the lens of social and environmental justice.

In 2017, Paul Hawken published the international bestseller *Drawdown: The Most Comprehensive Plan Ever Proposed to Reverse Global Warming* with the intention of moving the conversation away from despair to a sense of possibility. Hawken believes we have focused too much on the problems and not on the solutions. Working with a team of experts across many disciplines, he offers a blueprint that ranges from the need to phase out HFC refrigerants to the education and empowerment of women.

He believes too that we must overcome our tendency to think in silos. In a 2019 interview for non-profit Bioneers, he said, "We have to be careful that we do not fall into a conceptual trap that we need to 'fix' the climate. This is the same thinking that broke it, making the atmosphere something separate and 'other.' What we need to transform is how we relate to life down here, both nature and each other. Social justice is at the heart of regeneration and our ability to reverse the climate crisis. Othering Indigenous people, races, religions, regions and nature is the fundamental disease of our time."

Movement visionaries

I also find hope in forward-looking projects and movements that are changing the way we look at human rights and the rights of the planet itself. David Boyd is a Canadian environmental lawyer and professor of law, policy and sustainability at the University of British Columbia as well as the UN special rapporteur on human rights and the environment. In his many reports and books, he has clearly shown how people living in polluted or compromised environments are often denied their human rights and even suffer abuse when they try to confront the government or industry responsible.

Boyd is a passionate advocate of codifying the human right to a healthy environment into law. In an October 2020 blog for the Canadian environmental justice group Ecojustice, Boyd says that in a time of global threat, it is more important than ever for all governments to recognize and protect the human right to a safe and healthy environment. "This means everyone having access to clean air, a safe climate, healthy ecosystems and biodiversity, being able to live and work in a non-toxic environment with clean water and sanitation and having access to healthy and sustainably produced food. By enshrining and upholding the right to a healthy environment, the most vulnerable have the ability to hold those in power accountable."

This concept of climate justice is key to fighting the climate crisis. There are hundreds of climate-based legal challenges being launched by civil society organizations around the world, and Greenpeace has said that climate justice is the fulfillment of human rights in the face of existential threat. "It is a process of addressing the climate crisis as a human rights crisis and using the court of law to hold corporations and governments accountable." In an email to me Boyd adds, "The power of a rights-based approach to climate change is that it transforms unenforceable environmental commitments, such as those made under the Paris Agreement, into legally binding obligations. We have witnessed this powerful merger of environmental law and human rights law in pioneering Supreme Court decisions from Colombia to the Netherlands, with courts finding that inadequate government action to address the climate crisis violates human rights."

There has been great progress. Today, 156 of 193 UN member states recognize the right to a healthy environment through constitutional amendments, legislation and court decisions, and at least a thousand civil society organizations called for its recognition at the UN. In an

October 2021 historic decision, the UN Human Rights Council formally recognized — for the first time — that having a clean, healthy and sustainable environment is a basic human right. Boyd says this pact would increase accountability and require that every country do its part to protect its people from the impacts of pollution, toxic substances, the climate crisis and biodiversity loss.

Ecojustice welcomed this decision and said it would put pressure on the government of Canada to recognize the right to a healthy environment. The government is reforming the Canadian Environmental Protection Act (CEPA), the country's cornerstone environmental law, not updated in over 20 years. In supporting the Canadian government's stated intent to include the right to a healthy environment in an updated CEPA, Ecojustice and other environmental groups point to a report for the UN by Baskut Tuncak, former UN special rapporteur on hazardous substances and wastes. Tuncak toured Canada's pollution hot spots and noted that many were near racialized and Indigenous communities. He reported that the lack of a legal right to a healthy environment has a direct and negative impact on many vulnerable communities and strongly recommended that Canada adopt legislation to rectify this.

But things are moving. Canada is poised to adopt a private members' bill that calls for a national strategy to redress environmental racism by examining the link between race, socio-economic status and environmental risk. The strategy would also assess the need for new laws and policies to protect vulnerable communities. In

2016, Canada endorsed the United Nations Declaration on the Rights of Indigenous Peoples (UNDRIP) and in December 2020 introduced legislation that commits the government to "take all measures necessary to ensure that the laws of Canada are consistent with the rights of Indigenous peoples set out in the Declaration as well as to develop an action plan to achieve its objects."

UNDRIP is important because it establishes a universal framework of minimum standards for the survival, dignity and well-being of Indigenous peoples and elaborates on existing human rights standards and fundamental freedoms. Importantly, it goes beyond past human rights advances that tended to be based on the notion of individual rights and moves toward a more collective approach to human rights.

These rights are key to fighting climate destruction. The deep Indigenous connection to the land and other living beings should be our template for planetary healing. American environmentalist, educator and author David W. Orr says we will not fight to protect what we do not love. Western culture has long viewed man and nature as separate. Indigenous teachings show us a more unified world view. Terri-Lynn Williams-Davidson, Elizabeth Bulbrook and Nigel Baker-Grenier are lawyers with the Haida Nation legal firm White Raven Law. In a November 2019 guest blog for Environmental Defence, they explained why Indigenous rights are a crucial part of climate action, using the example of the Haida people, who have had a presence on an archipelago off the coast of British Columbia for at least 12,500 years. "The Haida are bound to the land and the sea through reciprocal relationships reflected in Haida law. These relationships acknowledge the interconnectivity of human beings, the lands and waters of Haida Gwaii, plants, animals, and supernatural beings. . . . The Haida have a responsibility to care for the land and manage it in a way that is sustainable for all future generations. In return, Haida Gwaii provides rich resources which enable the Haida people to thrive. UNDRIP affirms Indigenous Peoples' role in environmental protection, and for the Haida, that role is grounded in Haida laws, values, and world view."

Recognizing the rights of nature

Another growing movement seeks to protect the natural world in law. The Universal Declaration of the Rights of Mother Earth was created at an international civil society summit in Bolivia after the failure of the 2009 intergovernmental climate summit in Copenhagen. The declaration recognizes that the Earth is an indivisible living community of interrelated and interdependent beings with inherent rights. The Global Alliance on the Rights of Nature (GARN), where I serve on the advisory board, is an international alliance of grassroots groups, Indigenous communities, organizations and individuals committed to the universal adoption and implementation of legal systems that recognize, respect and enforce the rights of nature. We believe that we humans have to balance what is good for us against what is good for the planet as a whole. It is the holistic recognition that all life, all ecosystems on our planet are intertwined.

In his groundbreaking 2011 book, *Wild Law*, South African lawyer Cormac Cullinan wrote that future generations will look back on ours and view our relationship with nature as a form of slavery. He writes, "The day will come when the failure of our laws to recognize the right of a river to flow, to prohibit acts that destabilize the Earth's climate, or to impose a duty to respect the intrinsic value and right of all life will be as reprehensible as allowing people to be bought and sold." Most legal jurisdictions view nature as property and most laws to protect the environment and other species regulate only the amount of damage that can be inflicted by human activity, rather than regulating human behaviour in a manner that allows other species to fulfill their evolutionary role on the planet.

In his 2017 book, *The Rights of Nature: A Legal Revolution That Could Save the World*, David Boyd explains that the intent of this campaign is not to impose a human-rights framework on nature, but rather to give legal recognition of the rights of animal species and ecosystems to survive and thrive. No one is saying you cannot fish. But to fish a species to extinction should be forbidden.

GARN instituted the International Rights of Nature Tribunal to adjudicate social and environmental justice cases within the framework of a rights-of-nature jurisprudence. We have held tribunals at most of the annual governmental climate summits and the findings and recommendations from the tribunals are widely published. The European Tribunal in Defence of Aquatic Ecosystems, chaired by Cormac Cullinan, was held virtually during

2021 and heard testimonies on the melting of Europe's glaciers; water contamination in Lake Vettern, Sweden; hydroelectric dams in the Balkans and bauxite contamination in Marseille. Its recommendations are pending.

There have been many breakthroughs expanding legal protections. Ecuador and Bolivia have both amended their constitutions to enshrine the rights of nature. In 2017, New Zealand's courts recognized the Whanganui River as a rights-bearing entity, with the rights, duties and liabilities of a legal person, setting a new legal precedent. The local Maori people and government representatives are joint caretakers of the river.

Months later, Colombia's constitutional court approved legal rights for the Atrato River near the Panama border. A year later, the country's supreme court acknowledged the legal rights of the Amazonian ecosystems in a lawsuit brought forward by 25 young people. Using the New Zealand case as an example, a court in the northern Indian state of Uttarakhand granted the Ganges and its major tributary, the Yamuna, the status of living human entities. Australia has adopted a law that recognizes the Yarra River's rights as a living entity, and in July 2019, the supreme court of Bangladesh proclaimed all of the nation's rivers to be alive and entitled to legal rights. While contamination continues to plague many waterways, these developments are a crucial first step in a process of creating law to truly protect nature.

In the US, dozens of communities have adopted citizen ordinances declaring their right to protect local parks, lakes and wetlands. The legal status of these local initiatives is not clear, but the notion that local communities should have such rights is growing, as are the movements behind them. In 2016, the residents of Toledo, Ohio, fed up with constant blue-green algae pollution of their drinking water from Lake Erie, launched the Lake Erie Bill of Rights campaign that would allow citizens to bring lawsuits on behalf of Lake Erie instead of having to depend on governments or regulatory agencies clearly not doing their job. Four years later, the City of Toledo voted in favour of the bill, but an industrialized agriculture company filed a lawsuit arguing the bill was detrimental to its business and had it ruled unconstitutional. The fight continues.

In February 2021, backed by the community, the local Innu Council of Ekuanitshit in Côte-Nord, northern Quebec, granted legal personhood to the Magpie River, an internationally renowned whitewater rafting site that winds nearly 300 kilometres before it empties into the St. Lawrence River. As the *National Observer* notes, the river already has a major hydroelectric dam on it and the community wants to protect it from further disruption.

This is a concrete example of Indigenous values and culture joining the larger global movement to recognize the rights of nature, and in accordance with Innu customs and practices, the river has been granted the rights to flow, to be respected in its cycles, to protect and preserve its natural evolution, to maintain its natural biodiversity, to fulfill its essential functions within its ecosystem; to maintain its integrity; to be safe from pollution, to regenerate and be restored and to sue. Innu Council Chief Jean-Charles Piétacho said that his people are not the owners of the river but its protectors, and will now have more authority to fulfill this obligation. L'Observatoire international des droits de la nature, a Quebec-based coalition, is now lobbying governments to give personhood rights to the mighty St. Lawrence River.

Growing food to regenerate the planet

Another community-based movement is leading us to a more sustainable way to produce food. The dominant model of chemical-dependent, mass-produced industrial farming is a source of carbon emissions, serious air and water pollution and soil destruction. It is equally destructive of communities, as many farms are now giant business operations with corporate ownership. UN scientists warn that the planet has only 60 years of farming left if soil degradation from industrial farming continues. A few corporations own and control entire crop varieties, from seed to table, promoting monoculture and dictating farm policies to governments.

Factory farming animals is enormously harmful as well, but the European Union is stepping up efforts to control wildlife trading and make animal farming more sustainable and humane, given that both issues have played a role in the coronavirus pandemic, EU environment commissioner Virginijus Sinkevičius said in a April 2020 interview with Reuters. Recent animal welfare reform measures in Europe are promising and include better animal welfare labelling, the promise of an inquiry on the transport of live animals inside the EU, and the historic decision to end caged animal farming taken in July 2021. Reacting to public pressure, Switzerland has promised a public vote on a full ban on factory farming. The UK has recognized animals as sentient beings and banned both the export of live animals and the import of hunting trophies, ivory and shark fins.

In the US, Senator Cory Booker has introduced legislation to phase out factory farms. Food & Water Watch says his Farm System Reform Act will include reforms that will make it possible for independent family-scale producers to make a fair living. They include a moratorium on large factory farms, a buy-out package for existing ones to be shut down by 2040, and the holding of big agricultural corporations responsible for the waste, pollution, public health consequences and property value declines for which they are responsible.

Regenerative farming, on the other hand, works with nature to restore soil and natural water systems. It seeks to rehabilitate and enhance the entire ecosystem of a farm by placing a premium on soil health through biodiversity, crop rotation, natural grazing, rainwater harvesting, mulching and, crucially, the restoration and retention of watersheds. By restoring soil and greening the lands, rain returns, creating healthy local hydraulic cycles.

Regeneration International is a network of more than 250 international partners that work to facilitate and accelerate the global transition to regenerative food, farming and land management for the purpose of restoring climate stability, ending world hunger and rebuilding deteriorating social and economic systems. Regeneration movements are springing up in communities around the world and many companies, including some major brands, have pledged to produce their products on land where regenerative agriculture is being practised.

At home, the non-profit Regeneration Canada brings together farmers, landowners, scientists, agronomists and community groups dedicated to farming techniques that mimic natural ecosystems to maximize soil health and sequester carbon. Farmers for Climate Solutions is another Canadian alliance of farmers and supporters who believe that agriculture must be part of the solution to the climate crisis. Noting that the food-producing sector is responsible for 12% of the country's greenhouse gas emissions, the group says tackling climate change is an opportunity for farmers to create systems that are productive, provide sustainable livelihoods and protect the environment. But farmers need help, as many are often in debt.

The group was very pleased that the April 2021 federal budget allocated over $320 million to programs to help famers reduce agricultural greenhouse gases and store carbon. Said National Farmers Union president Katie Ward, "The federal government listened to farm organizations and farmer-led coalitions and brought forward important programs that will help us reduce our emissions. With these programs, farmers will be empowered to make changes, cut emissions, and contribute to Canada's goal of reducing GHGs by 30% by 2030."

Some hope in the war on plastic

The World Economic Forum says the world is entering a new era in its relationship with plastic. For a long time, plastic was a miracle product — it was cheap and light and revolutionized safe food storage; it helped save lives in the health sector and, more recently, facilitated the manufacture of wind turbines and solar panels. Its success has led to a vast quantity of plastic waste over the last 60 years and has become "public enemy number one," says the forum.

While the statistics on plastics use are grim, much is being done to stop and eventually reverse the damage. The United Nations says that as of 2018, 127 countries had implemented some type of restriction on plastic bags. India pledged in 2018 to eliminate all single-use plastic in the country by 2022. China has announced plans to phase out most single-use plastic bags and straws by 2025, the largest country to commit to such measures. Kenya, Chile and Morocco have banned plastic bags. The European Union has vowed to ban single-use cutlery, cotton swabs, straws and stir-sticks as well as single-use polystyrene cups. Plastic water bottles must be made of 25% recycled content by 2025 and 90% by 2029. Canada and the United Kingdom announced similar pledges to ban single-use plastic in 2020 and plastic is now considered toxic under the revised Canadian Environmental Protection Act, a move long sought by environmentalists and opposed by the country's $28-billion plastics industry.

Many cities have banned some single-use plastic as well. New York City, Los Angeles, San Francisco and Miami

Beach have all banned plastic straws, a major source of coastal pollution. In 2018, World Wildlife Fund launched Plastic Smart Cities; a global city initiative to eliminate municipal plastic waste from nature by 2030. Since then, dozens of cities have joined the project and are developing action plans. Fifteen cities in Asia have committed to a 30% reduction in plastic leakage by 2025 and key cities on the Mediterranean have committed to ambitious targets to avoid plastic leakage into this already polluted sea. Industry is getting the strong consumer message. Two hundred and fifty major brands recently pledged to cut plastic waste altogether from their operations. The pledge was signed by all three of the worst plastics polluters: Coca-Cola, PepsiCo and Nestlé.

Much of this action has been driven by the many civil society organizations and community groups fighting for a plastics-free world. Break Free from Plastic is an international movement committed to a world "where the land, sky, oceans and water is home to an abundance of life, not an abundance of plastic, and where the air we breathe, the water we drink and the food we eat is free of toxic by-products of plastic pollution." Launched in 2016, it already has close to 2,000 member organizations. Washington-based Plastic Pollution Coalition has a campaign to get Amazon to stop using single-use plastic packaging and is reaching out to the company's 100 million customers to join them in this demand.

And the Nordic countries — Denmark, Finland, Iceland, Norway and Sweden — have teamed up with World Wildlife Fund to propose a global treaty to stop plastic pollution of the oceans. *Plasteurope*, an industry journal, quotes Guðmunder Ingi Guðbrandsson, Iceland's environment minister, who said, "Plastics pollution does not respect borders. That is why this is an international task, like most other environmental challenges. Such issues need to be dealt with by global agreements and strong actions in each country. Our task now is to reach consensus on a new global agreement. This is not a question of when, but how. We must not waste any time."

The Guardian reports that there is international support for such a treaty. A UN working group on marine litter and microplastics met in November 2020 and announced that more than two-thirds of UN member states have declared they are open to an agreement. A resolution calling for the world's nations to agree to a binding global agreement was adopted by the International Union for the Conservation of Nature and millions have signed the petition supporting the call. In July 2021, scientists from around the world published a call in the journal *Science* for the global treaty to end production of virgin plastic by 2040.

Now we must challenge the old narrative

The success of these and other initiatives requires that we continue to challenge the culture and tenets of economic globalization, because its core imperative is the drive for unlimited growth. The growth imperative — the very heart of unregulated capitalism — dictates that, to succeed, more is always better. Governments measure their success by their gross domestic product (the monetary value of all goods and services they produce) and by their balance of trade. Corporations must produce and sell more than their competitors, and this means cutting more trees, extracting more raw materials and shipping more goods over longer distances, generating a greater energy footprint. Simply put, the growth imperative is at war with the survival of our planet. Thankfully there are communities and organizations driving a demand for deep structural reform of the global economy and who it serves, especially in the wake of COVID-19.

COVID exposed deep inequality, both between and within countries. While the virus was a threat to all who came in contact with it, poor and racialized people were more likely to be performing the kinds of jobs that exposed them to greater risk and to be living in more crowded homes and communities where it was harder to maintain physical distancing. Access to good health care for those who were infected varied dramatically around the world and vaccine nationalism meant that wealthy countries inoculated their populations first.

The pandemic has opened our eyes to the dangers of falling back on the economic and social system that failed in so many ways. In an October 2020 op-ed in *The Guardian*, six UN independent human rights experts said that the pandemic exposed the fallout of decades of global privatization and market competition. Vital public goods and services have been outsourced to private companies, or simply underfunded, leading to overwhelmed health systems and families struggling to keep safe, educate their children and make ends meet. Calling for a "radical change in direction," the experts wrote that the neoliberal construct of states taking a back seat to private companies must be abandoned.

"It is time to say it loud and clear: the commodification of health, education, housing, water, sanitation and other rights-related resources and services prices out the poor and may result in violations of human rights. States can no longer cede control as they have done. They are not absolved of their human rights obligations by delegating core goods and services to private companies and the market on terms that they know will effectively undermine the rights and livelihoods of many people. . . . This is also a pivotal moment for the human rights community. We call on all those committed to human rights to address the consequences of privatisation head on. Human rights can help articulate the public goods and services we want — participatory, transparent, sustainable, accountable, non-discriminatory and serving the common good."

There is evidence that governments have heard this call. Management consulting firm McKinsey & Company reported that by the end of 2020, massive government spending has reversed the long-term trend of institutional pullback in the social contract. G20 countries alone launched fiscal packages exceeding US$10 trillion, 30 times the size of the post Second World War Marshall Plan that helped rebuild Europe. This does not include President Biden's March 2021 "Rescue Plan" to combat COVID-19, the climate crisis and racial inequality and invest in the expansion of the public health-care workforce and the frayed social safety net.

Nnimmo Bassey

Nnimmo Bassey is a Nigerian activist, poet and architect. He is the director of the ecological think tank Health of Mother Earth Foundation, a member of the steering committee of Oilwatch International and former chair of Friends of the Earth International. He is an internationally known leader for environmental justice.

What gives you hope?

"A lifetime of activism has taught me that there is no end to learning. The lesson I learn every day is never to think the job has been done just because one battle had been won. What of the battles being fought by the oppressed elsewhere? What of the battles being fought by insects, animals and birds trapped in wildfires set by humans? Until and unless we regain our memory, our humanity, our being children of Mother Earth, we get entrapped by the fictional powers of capital and remain a long way from home. We can only understand nature when we see ourselves as a fraction of who she is.

"A lifetime of pondering the poetics of life has taught me never to lose hope. It has taught me to be attentive to sights, to smells and to sounds, as they are all markers of life. I am enamoured of the sounds of struggles. The inspiring music of the thumping of resolute steps and dripping sweat from unified hands linked and pushing forward demands of justice, fairness and dignity. Above all, I keep in view the truth that we must never give up until love overcomes hate and solidarity trumps division.

"Through acts of solidarity and counternarratives, vulnerable peoples have stood strong and defeated powerful corporations and oppressive institutions and governments. Along the way, we have learned that life is not all about winning. Our struggles and the hopes we inspire enrich our lives and provide scaffolds for the construction of preferred futures."

Clearly this is harder for the poorer countries and regions of the Global South. But there are hopeful signs of understanding that to help them invest in desperately needed public services, the debt burden must be lifted. More than 100 organizations joined Oxfam and ActionAid International in April 2020, calling for debt payments to be dropped to free up more than US$25 billion that could go to caring for people in the Global South.

The World Council of Churches, representing 500 million Christians, says that scarce resources are directed away from lifesaving public health and social service systems toward debt payments and has joined other faith-based communities to call for G20 governments and financial institutions to release countries from this debt burden. United Nations Secretary-General Guterres has called on the World Bank and the International Monetary Fund to grant a debt standstill for all poor nations, warning of economic collapse in many, and both have responded with promises of a comprehensive plan of debt relief.

Toward an Earth- and human-centred economy

Like Paul Hawken's "shadow world" that strode into the WTO ministerial meeting in Seattle, a new vision for a different set of values to guide us is emerging. COVID-19 and the environmental crisis are the twin threats that have forced us to re-evaluate the growth imperative and the power of the market to make decisions that affect our everyday lives.

COVID reminded us that we must share and cooperate to survive. Communities have found ways to reach out to their most vulnerable members. Calls for improvements in long-term care facilities for seniors have led to improved regulations and a stronger role for governments in elder care. Watching frontline workers put themselves in danger has led to public support for a living wage. There is a more urgent campaign to provide sanitation for the billions without. The failure of global supply chains to provide essential medical supplies has forced governments to play a greater role in protecting their citizens. Calls for an end of corporate rule and capitalism itself are growing as is the demand for an enhanced and positive role for the state.

COVID-19 exposed the obscene gaps in wealth and opportunity. In March 2021, the Inequality Project of the Washington-based Institute for Policy Studies reported that global billionaire wealth surged by US$4 trillion in the first year of the pandemic. This led to a growing demand for a surtax on the wealthy and a clampdown on tax havens. The International Monetary Fund called on advanced economies to use more progressive income taxes, inheritance and property taxes and taxes on "excess" corporate profits to help reduce inequalities exposed by COVID-19. In a move that would have been unthinkable even a few years ago, at their October 30, 2021 meeting, G20 leaders endorsed Joe Biden's call for a 15% minimum global corporate tax to stop transnational corporations from shifting their profits to low-tax havens.

In "Economics for the People," an October 2020 essay for the digital magazine *Aeon*, Duke University economic historian Dirk Philipsen says our current system, which he terms "the tragedy of the private," imposes an ideology that puts private interest above the common good. Philipsen acknowledges that the system of economic growth has generated unprecedented wealth and knowledge but says we live in a different world now. What might have been justified in the past to overcome poverty and scarcity no longer holds sway in a world where we do not need "more," rather "better and more fairly distributed."

Living in the midst of a historic transition, he writes, it is our great fortune that we still have a choice. Priorities should include regulations preventing the violation of critical ecological thresholds, repairing egregious market failures, valuing essential workers, providing basic services and incomes for all and a basic moral recognition that nothing — not race, not nation, not gender, not personal contributions, not your zip code — should ever be a legitimate cause for either extreme poverty or excessive wealth. "It is time to rewrite the script," Philipsen says. "It is now time to make our exceptional human capacity to create and cooperate part of our governance structures — part of the operating logic of modern societies. Perhaps then we can bring to life what others could only envision: a system focused on well-being of people and planet, liberating our individual and collective capabilities."

Oxford economist Kate Raworth would agree with this. Her 2017 bestseller, *Doughnut Economics: Seven Ways to Think Like a 21st-Century Economist*, proposes an alternative economic system to untrammelled capitalism, one that balances essential human needs and planetary boundaries. Raworth says that 20th-century thinking is not equipped to deal with life in the 21st and a climate in crisis. The outer ring of her doughnut-shaped model represents the nine ecological limits of Earth's life-supporting systems that humanity must not overshoot. Its inner ring represents the baseline for 12 essentials of life, including food, water, health and social equality. The space between the two rings, which Raworth calls the sweet spot, is both environmentally safe and socially just. Getting into the doughnut is meant to replace the current emphasis on GDP growth.

A number of cities are adopting Raworth's model and setting out to adapt it in a way suitable to their unique circumstances. In a January 2021 story, *Time* correspondent Ciara Nugent reports that Amsterdam has embraced this model, with plans to bring all 872,000 residents inside the doughnut. Plans include a large infrastructure investment, a major new employment project, major recycling and retooling of materials, and new policies for government contracts. Working with the grassroots coalition of some 400 people and groups, Amsterdam officials note that doughnut thinking is part of their DNA now. Marieke van Doorninck, deputy mayor for sustainability and urban planning, told Nugent that Raworth had already told them what to do but, COVID-19 showed them the way: "I think in the darkest times, it's easiest to imagine another world."

Many voices are calling for deep structural reform of international institutions. Progressive International is a global initiative launched in 2020 to promote progressive ideas and movements. Two founding members, Yanis Varoufakis, former finance minister of Greece, and David Adler, political economist and former adviser to

Senator Bernie Sanders, say we should not rush to save or kill the old liberal order but remake it. In a December 2018 op-ed for *The Guardian*, they remind us that the International Monetary Fund (IMF) and the World Bank were conceived as agents of change and could be again. To write them off leaves us in a vacuum. The IMF should oversee an international monetary clearing union that rebalances the current gross capital and trade imbalances.

The World Bank should oversee a Green New Deal in collaboration with public investment banks, aided by coordinated interventions in the bond market by central banks.

20th-century thinking is not equipped to deal with life in the 21st and a climate in crisis.

The authors are also critical of the International Labour Organization (ILO), formed in 1919 with a radical vision of international solidarity for workers. A century later, it is at once more needed and more absent than ever, having lost its political salience and all but disappeared from the political vocabulary. The ILO should have the power to investigate countries that suppress workers and unions as well as corporations that fail to comply with international labour standards. Adler and Varoufakis also propose a new institution, a Tax Justice Authority, to eliminate tax evasion.

The IMF certainly appears to be listening. In an October 2020 report called *Fiscal Monitor: Policies for the Recovery*, it concluded that the economic benefits of market-based policies designed to shrink or contain the size of government had been badly oversold, while the social and economic costs had been significantly underestimated and led to increased inequality. The IMF called upon governments to dramatically increase public investments to revive economic activity after "the deepest and sharpest economic collapse in contemporary history." Public investments in transportation, water services, health care, schools, safe buildings, roads and bridges would create millions of jobs and "lay the foundation for a more resilient economy by investing in job-rich, highly productive, and greener activities." The IMF expressed skepticism that private investment can play as important a role as the public — a sharp turn from its historical allegiance to the market.

In a September 2019 report, the UN Conference on Trade and Development has taken the visionary position that the only way to meet the ambitious pledges of the UN's 2030 Social Development Goals is for the world to find the political will to change the rules of the international economic game. Governments must make a clean break with the years of austerity and scale up the resources needed for a big investment push led by the public sector to help bring about a more equal distribution of income and reverse decades of environmental degradation.

Over 600 labour, consumer, environmental and other civil society organizations are pushing for reform of the World Trade Organization (WTO). In a spring 2021 open letter to all heads of state, they noted how badly equipped the WTO was to handle the economic crisis brought on by the pandemic and that this is an opportune time to reform the institution and its priorities. "The choice is not between the status quo or no trade. That is a straw man hawked by those who want nothing to change. Change is happening. The question is what multilateral framework can be inclusive, promote real sustainability, human rights and prosperity for all, and deliver the benefits of expanded trade to most people, while also providing our elected representatives the policy space to promote the public interest."

Change is happening.

There is also progress being made toward an internationally binding treaty that will hold transnational corporations accountable for their many abuses. In 2014 the UN Human Rights Council adopted a resolution, long promoted by human rights organizations, to create a legal instrument that would ensure transnational corporations respect human rights and it established an intergovernmental working group to develop it. Lucia Ortiz, economic justice coordinator for Friends of the Earth International, says the time has come for a full treaty. "A treaty would also give victims of corporate abuses access to justice where there is none and challenge the economic and political power of transnational corporations." Support is growing, with many cities around the world now advocating for a binding treaty and 94 countries — mostly from the Global South — supporting a draft treaty drawn up by Ecuador and South Africa in 2018. They feel it is only a matter of time until they will be successful.

On January 22, 2021, the UN Treaty on the Prohibition of Nuclear Weapons entered into force, backed by 130 countries and already ratified by 51. The treaty requires ratifying nations to "never under any circumstances develop, test, produce, manufacture, otherwise acquire, possess or stockpile nuclear weapons or other nuclear explosive devices." This was a huge victory for the many people and organizations that have been advocating for a nuclear-free world for years. There are nearly 14,000 nuclear weapons in the world possessed by just nine countries and Greenpeace estimates that the cost of these weapons over the last decade is close to US$1,000 billion.

Stockholm-based Right Livelihood acknowledged that the states that did not sign the treaty are not bound by it but point out that they have a legal obligation under the UN Charter to achieve security without relying on the threat of force in their international relations. "If we have learned anything from the climate crisis, unprecedented biodiversity loss and the COVID-19 pandemic, it is that militarism and weapons, including nuclear weapons, are useless in addressing the key human security issues of today and tomorrow."

New hope in Canada

There are similar calls for deep transformation of the economy and political culture in Canada. Alex Himelfarb, York University professor and former clerk of the Privy Council, says the COVID-19 pandemic updated the fiscal approach to austerity that has led federal policy in Canada since the mid-1980s. The federal government invested hugely in helping Canadians fight the virus and recover from the economic fallout of layoffs and closings. And it went further into debt as the pandemic ended to kickstart recovery and address the cracks in the system that it had exposed. Himelfarb notes, as does economist Jim Stanford, that Canada's fiscal situation is the envy of most countries and that rising public debt is entirely manageable if interest rates remain low and the Bank of Canada continues to buy federal and provincial bonds. He points out that the debt level after the Second World War was very high but a booming economy overtook it.

Canadians for Tax Fairness says the government should introduce new taxes targeting extreme wealth concentration and use the revenues to strengthen social safety nets and stimulate the economy. Canada is the only G7 country without a wealth, inheritance or estate tax, the organization points out, and this has allowed extreme wealth to accumulate at the top. In a March 2021 report for the Canadian Centre for Policy Alternatives, Alex Himelfarb says a 1% tax on wealth over $20 million would generate about $10 billion in revenues in its first year, which in turn could be used to lift thousands out of poverty and to implement increased funding for important social programs such as child and senior care. A moderately more ambitious wealth tax could raise double that amount. A November 2020 survey by Abacus Data found that a majority of Canadians (79%) favour a wealth tax and this support crosses party lines.

In August 2021, Abacus Research conducted a poll for the Broadbent Institute and the Professional Institute for the Public Service of Canada. It found that 57% of Canadians believe the pandemic increased inequality,

70% want a more equitable tax system, 88% support a wealth tax and 92% do not want the government to cut essential services and health care to pay for deficit and recovery.

Increased calls are also coming for trade policy reform in Canada. The Trudeau government has never seen a trade agreement it didn't like, but the times have changed. COVID-19 wreaked havoc with global supply chains and governments everywhere implemented domestic programs and supported domestic industry where needed, often in violation of trade rules. President Biden completely ignored the new Canada–United States–Mexico Agreement when he launched his ambitious Buy America plan and cancelled the Keystone Pipeline. And the massive stimulus package the Trudeau government launched to rebuild public services and invest directly in the domestic economy may very well violate trade agreements that are intended to hand over major policy decisions to the market. In a March 2021 report for the Canadian Centre for Policy Alternatives, Lucinda Chitapain, a trade specialist with the Montreal law firm McCarthy Tétrault, warned that in the context of COVID-19, government restrictions setting price controls over health equipment and giving emergency support to domestic businesses could all give rise to costly investor-state dispute settlement suits.

The National Union of Public Government Employees is calling for a serious discussion about alternatives to the existing trade model, one that allows us to redevelop our productive capacity and create good jobs in Canada. We have given up important tools, such as preference for

Canadian producers, direct financial assistance and public ownership. Economist Jim Stanford says trade deals should be limited to reducing tariffs, facilitating trade promotion and trade infrastructure and harmonizing product standards while respecting genuine safety and environmental goals.

And all political parties are now committed — at least on paper — to a serious climate strategy. In his 2020 bestseller, *A Good War: Mobilizing Canada for the Climate Emergency*, Seth Klein, former director of the British Columbia office of the Canadian Centre for Policy Alternatives, argues that Canada needs to look to the way it mobilized for the Second World War to deal with the climate crisis. He said strong wartime government leadership "took the public where they needed to go" by establishing an "emergency mindset"; rallying the public at every turn; creating common cause across race, class and gender; embracing economic planning; spending what it takes to win and reintegrating those negatively affected by the effort into the workforce. During the war, Klein points out, Canada shifted to full employment, remaking the economy to mobilize against an existential threat. We, and the rest of the planet, face another such threat now and must commit to the same level of mobilization.

In a June 2020 interview with Linda Solomon Wood of the *National Observer*, Nature Canada's Graham Saul expressed optimism because he sees real opportunity for social movements to win victories on the climate crisis and in other areas. He has called for a "Canadian Nature Corps" to get people out of their homes and into nature to restore wetlands and grasslands, rebuild coastal ecosystems, replant over scars left behind by unused logging roads and retrofit visitor centres, camping grounds, trails and other infrastructure in urban and rural parks. We can put thousands of people to work combatting invasive species and reclaiming habitat of endangered wildlife, Saul says, and take joy in doing so. "It's really easy to just be fundamentally depressed all the time. But the reality is that good things do happen, progress does get made. And while we have a long struggle, we need to find a way to celebrate the victories as we go along."

Pollster Michael Adams documented a trend coming out of the turbulence of the last few years in a poll to see if Canadian values on inclusiveness had changed after a time of "exceptional stress, illness and death and brutal economic fall-out." He published his findings in a January 2021 *Globe and Mail* editorial. While populists around the world used the pandemic to sow fears against newcomers, were Canadians drawn to messages that blame "the other"? Did we see a growing hostility to immigrants, to minority groups or voices of dissent such as those of environmental activists? A resounding no, no, no and no, reports Adams. In fact, Canada has never been more sure of its welcoming spirit than now, he reported. A majority of Canadians see immigrants as good for the country, not as threats. Adams says that Canadians are now more accepting of immigrants than he has seen in four decades of polling.

How does this square with the growing reports of acts of race-based hate? Adams acknowledges this rise in racist incidents but says they have had the opposite effect of their mission. As Canadians have learned more about these experiences, their attitudes have been changing not toward more denial but to greater empathy. There has been a "drastic decline" in the proportion of Canadians who claim racism is not a problem here. Canadians are increasingly convinced of the seriousness of systemic inequities and sympathetic to the efforts of those who are working to redress them.

There is also a growing desire on the part of Canadians to see their governments be more proactive in advancing reconciliation with Indigenous peoples. A June 2021 national survey conducted by the Environics Institute showed increased support among non-Indigenous Canadians for Indigenous rights and reconciliation over previous years. A growing proportion also recognize that they have a role to play as individuals in efforts to bring about true reconciliation. The discovery of the bodies of thousands of Indigenous children buried at residential schools caused an outcry from people and organizations across the political spectrum and are likely to enhance the call for justice.

Adams also reported changes in attitudes toward who has too much power in Canada and who has too little. Large majorities say that the wealthy and large corporations have too much influence over politics and that environmental groups, feminists, ethnic minorities and Indigenous peoples all have too little. Not only do most Canadians agree that minority interests are Canadian interests, they are also increasingly sympathetic to vulnerable groups such as people with low incomes. And Canadians support strong public services. Nine in ten agree that all Canadians should have access to high-quality public services such as health care and education. This ideology shapes our political culture, says Adams.

This feels like hope to me. And it feels like the stage of Bill Moyer's Movement Action Plan where we have mobilized broad public support in Canada, and in many places around the world, for fundamental change.

The pandemic gave us a collective shock that has the ability to produce real change. We know we cannot stay on our planet-destroying path. We now truly understand the need to ensure public health at a global level and that means it cannot be profit driven. The fight for human rights and racial, religious and gender equality has entered a crucial new stage and is widely supported. Public appreciation for working people and their unions has never been higher as we commit to class justice as well. The rise of right-wing populism in North America and Europe has stalled and the tenets of economic globalization — free trade, privatization, deregulation, corporate rule and unlimited growth — have been discredited. The moment for transformative politics and movements has come. Never has there been a greater need for principled and informed activism — and hope.

AFTERWORD

*You can't go back and change the beginning, but you
can start where you are and change the ending.*

C.S. LEWIS

This book has been a personal journey, for it has reminded me of the possibility of the human spirit to change and thus for the world to change. I end it with a sure knowledge that we will only find our way by remembering what went wrong "in the beginning" and letting it guide what we must do now. Many in our modern world have viewed nature as a resource to fuel unlimited growth and to exploit for our pleasure, convenience and profit. This has led to the violence and inequality that such thinking breeds. From this have we built a system in peril.

To get ourselves out of this trap we must listen to the voices calling for us to transform our economies and institutions so that they serve people, promote healthy communities and reconnect us with the living planet that supports our lives and those of the other species with which we share it.

According to the United Nations, Indigenous peoples compose less than 5% of the world's population but manage or hold tenure over 25% of its land surface and protect 80% of global biodiversity. Gleb Raygorodetsky is a research fellow specializing in traditional knowledge with the POLIS Project on Ecological Governance at the University of Victoria. In a November 2018 report for *National Geographic*, he writes that as our collective understanding of the imperilled state of our planet grows, global discourse and policy are finally starting to acknowledge the role of Indigenous peoples and their traditional territories in biodiversity conservation and climate change resilience.

Raygorodetsky cites projects, such as the Indigenous Rangers in Australia and Indigenous Guardians in Canada, where Indigenous communities have been empowered to manage their territories according to traditional law and in a way that advances national biodiversity conservation goals. Jon Waterhouse, Indigenous Peoples scholar with the Oregon Health and Science University and *National Geographic* Explorer, believes that we have lost our way and have forgotten what it means to have a relationship with the land. To find it again, we must follow the guides who have mastered the art of living on the Earth without destroying it.

We will have to "polish the art of seeing," according to Robin Wall Kimmerer, environmental and forest biology professor at State University of New York College and author of the 2013 book *Braiding Sweetgrass: Indigenous Wisdom, Scientific Knowledge and the Teachings of Plants.*

This means listening to plants and heeding the lessons of the natural world. "What would it be like, I wondered, to live with that heightened sensitivity to the lives given for ours? To consider the tree in the Kleenex, the algae in the toothpaste, the oaks in the floor, the grapes in the wine; to follow back the thread of life in everything and pay it respect? Once you start, it's hard to stop, and you begin to feel yourself awash in gifts."

I feel awash in the gift of such visionaries and in the community of activists here in Canada and around the world. We don't always know what will work and what will not. We get up in the morning and try. When we are at our best, we love and support one another and trust that our actions will make a difference. We embrace the world. And we are kind.

E. Ethelbert Miller, a much-loved African American poet and board chair of the Institute for Policy Studies, gives us this counsel:

"Place your heart in your hands and blow gently. Spread love like seed."

ACKNOWLEDGEMENTS

I am deeply grateful to amazing friends, colleagues, allies and comrades in the struggle for social and environmental justice here in Canada and around the world. Your inspiration and love have fed my soul.

Thank you to my thoughtful readers, Leo Broderick, Paul Moist and Fred Wilson. Thank you to the great team at ECW Press. Thank you to editors Jen Knoch and Susan Renouf. I listen to you because you are always right!

Thank you to my family and especially to Andrew for your ongoing love and support.

ENVIRONMENTAL BENEFITS STATEMENT

ECW Press Ltd saved the following resources by printing the pages of this book on chlorine free paper made with 100% post-consumer waste.

TREES	WATER	ENERGY	SOLID WASTE	GREENHOUSE GASES
38	**3,000**	**16**	**130**	**16,200**
FULLY GROWN	GALLONS	MILLION BTUs	POUNDS	POUNDS

Environmental impact estimates were made using the Environmental Paper Network Paper Calculator 4.0. For more information visit www.papercalculator.org

This book is also available as a Global Certified Accessible™ (GCA) ebook. ECW Press's ebooks are screen reader friendly and are built to meet the needs of those who are unable to read standard print due to blindness, low vision, dyslexia, or a physical disability.

At ECW Press, we want you to enjoy our books in whatever format you like. If you've bought a print copy just send an email to ebook@ecwpress.com and include:

- the book title
- the name of the store where you purchased it
- a screenshot or picture of your order/receipt number and your name
- your preference of file type: PDF (for desktop reading), ePub (for a phone/tablet, Kobo, or Nook), mobi (for Kindle)

A real person will respond to your email with your ebook attached. Please note this offer is only for copies bought for personal use and does not apply to school or library copies.

Thank you for supporting an independently owned Canadian publisher with your purchase!